What If I Name Her *Grace?*

Praise for
What If I Name Her Grace?

Chrissie's raw honesty about her journey as a new Christian mom is both inspiring and life-giving! Seeing Jesus come to life in a very "real life" kind of way as a mom, a wife, and a believer makes Him feel closer and more accessible than ever. Chrissie depicts the blossoming relationship of a new believer with the Lord in such an honest and relatable way. I definitely recommend this book to any woman who needs the reminder that she isn't alone and that Jesus is much nearer than we think.

Katie Chase,
wife, mom of two, entrepreneur, Christian

What If I Name Her Grace? is such a sweet memoir of an everyday wife and mom trying to grow closer to Jesus. In it, through Chrissie's telling of her varied life experiences, God proves time and time again that He is not only faithful, steady, and true, but also full of surprises, not the least of which being that He calls her to grow her family overseas. This book has strengthened my faith in God, especially when it comes to loving my neighbors who happen to live inside my house. Can't recommend it enough!

Lindsay Durrenberger,
Christian wife and mom, elementary teacher

This is the book I wish I had when my children were little. With a real-life understanding of the challenges and emotions moms experience, Chrissie shares wisdom and insights that inspire us to lean into our true source of strength, patience, and love so we can be the mothers we want to be. This book will become a trusted companion on your parenting journey. And with Chrissie's guidance, you'll likely find yourself offering more grace to yourself as well as to your family.

Laura Naiser,
Christian Mindset coach

This book paints an absolutely beautiful picture of God's grace and how it truly is sufficient for us. Chrissie's masterful writing powerfully shares the lessons God has taught her throughout her journey of motherhood. So relatable and uplifting. A must-read for any mama!

Rachel Perry,
Accountability and Mindset coach,
host of "Making the Leap" podcast

What an amazing gift this book is for young mothers, military wives, and any woman struggling with everyday life as a mom, wife, and child of God. Chrissie shares the story of how she renewed her relationship with God, and how that changed her life, her marriage, her ability to be the kind of mother she wanted to be, and even her health. It's a powerful story of how God uses ordinary moments in ordinary lives to create change that can last generations and affect everyone around us.

Nada Manley,
Christian stylist

Chrissie's journey to "grace" is a compelling story of a young military bride who had three children in six years and moved five times in nine years! Through all this, she found Christ and grace in her relationship with God and the Holy Spirit. Her journey not only included motherhood and all that it entails with very young children, but lifestyle changes in diet and exercise that improved her life and marriage and brought her a peaceful existence that enabled her to greet the dawn every day with prayer and study. This remarkable journey is not one on a superhighway, but a bumpy road with many moments of challenge: with her marriage, her children, and her faith. But succeed she did, and she brings to her state of grace encouragement and strength. *What If I Name Her Grace?* is a wonderful read that is truly inspiring.

Jeanne Kenaston,
author of *On Sabbatical, Volume 2: A Three Year, Round the World Sailing Adventure*

This book is so real, relevant, and inspiring for any person who reads it. The transparency of Chrissie's struggles and the lessons she learned gave me such grace for my own life as a mom with three young children. The book is laced with scriptures and spiritual concepts that both the baby and mature Christian can easily grasp. My self-perception as a Christian mother and wife has been impacted thanks to Chrissie's raw openness and confessions in her book.

Shareen Bender,
Christian mother of three girls birthed in three years

I was honored to be one of the first to read *What If I Name Her Grace?* It is a book of one family's raw journey of faith and learning to let go and let God. I recommend it to all young Christian wives and mothers who seek to make God the center of their home and life.

Becky Slaymaker,
Christian wife and mom

CHRISSIE KENASTON

What If I Name Her Grace?

How to Pursue Jesus Every Day &
Find God's Grace Even When You Miss the Mark

NASHVILLE

NEW YORK • LONDON • MELBOURNE • VANCOUVER

What If I Name Her Grace?

How to Pursue Jesus Every Day & Find God's Grace Even When You Miss the Mark

Published in New York, New York, by Morgan James Publishing. Morgan James is a trademark of Morgan James, LLC. www.MorganJamesPublishing.com

ISBN 9781631952975 paperback
ISBN 9781631952982 eBook
Library of Congress Control Number: 2020914888

Cover & Interior Design by:
Christopher Kirk
www.GFSstudio.com

Morgan James is a proud partner of Habitat for Humanity Peninsula and Greater Williamsburg. Partners in building since 2006.

Get involved today! Visit
MorganJamesPublishing.com/giving-back

For Michael, my rock, my best friend,
my leader, my perfect match.
Thank you for always bringing me back from the brink.

Contents

Foreword

P ursuing Jesus every day takes courage. It means showing up, ready to lean into Jesus with our whole self on both the good days and those crazy, awful, bad days. For me, that has meant being REAL with myself, not believing the lie that I am not enough or that I need to do more. Pursuing Jesus every day means letting go of the shame of not loving enough, of not having been present enough, of believing that I am just not enough. For some, it might mean the courage to bring disappointments and anger to Jesus. (He *understands* anger and the need to get it right!) For others, it might mean admitting the fear that sometimes grips a person to the point of thinking you don't have enough or know enough, and you never will.

My personal life verse comes from Romans 12:2 in The Message version. "So, here's what I want you to do, God helping you: Take your everyday, ordinary life—your sleeping, eating, going-to-work, and walking-around life—and place it before God as an offering. Embracing what God does for you is the best thing you can do for him." Notice the phrase "God helping you." This is not of our own strength. But with God's help and grace, we grow to become followers of Jesus and release the should-haves and ought-to's and live one day at a time.

Becoming a follower of Jesus doesn't happen overnight. It's an everyday, ordinary process, and most of the time it's not a neat and tidy process. Following Jesus is a slow process that takes time. Raising kids, being married, not being married, struggling with our past, longing for more in our future, being content, and becoming discontent are all a part of the process. It takes courage and patience and practice to become a Jesus follower. Then there are those days when we throw away everything we thought we knew and start all over again from scratch. Jesus takes us even closer into His arms and shows us an even deeper love. He provides a new lens through which to see those we love the most, but more importantly a new lens to see ourselves and begin to love ourselves as followers of Jesus.

This journey to pursue Jesus is not for the faint of heart. Those who choose this path will sometimes feel as though they are merely grasping the vine, and there is no way this vine will ever bear fruit. Thoughts of *There's no way my husband will ever have a personal relationship with Jesus* or *I doubt my children will ever know the love of God* can overwhelm us. Those thoughts may come true. But your personal choices to be faithful are pleasing to God. Say that again—the choices YOU make to remain faithful are pleasing to God. The Scriptures' invitation in John 15:5 is to "remain in me . . . because apart from me you can do nothing." It's hard not to try to control those around us on the journey. It's a great adrenalin rush to give others directions and correction along the way, but one of the hardest lessons I keep learning in my pursuit of Jesus is that I don't have control. God does! He is shaping me and refining me.

Through this book, Chrissie invites us to go on a journey of courage and growth. She shares with us what it really looks like in an everyday, ordinary life to pursue being a follower of Jesus. She shares with us the true depths of her heart as she tells stories of struggles with her marriage, her children, her faith, and her courage to remain in Him and cling to the Vine. As I read through this book, I couldn't help but relate to Chrissie's honest words of disappointment and struggle with her faith, but I also cried tears of joy as she told stories of overcoming some of the biggest hurdles in her marriage, raising her children, and her own self-doubt along the way. Chrissie gives us a glance inside the soul of a follower of Jesus as she learns to replace guilt and fear and anger with grace and forgiveness for others, but mostly for herself as she continually runs back into the arms of Jesus all along the way.

Teresa McCloy, follower of Jesus
coach, speaker, and creator of the REALIFE Process®
www.therealifeprocess.com

Introduction

I want to start by saying that I am *not* a Jesus know-it-all, and I do *not* judge anyone who lives or acts differently than I do. OK, whew! We got that out of the way. Christians can so often come across as judgmental, especially to nonbelievers, and I want to make it clear that that's never my intention. I am simply a Jesus-following wife and mom who wants to share her story.

I certainly don't have all the answers, but I've learned a lot in a short amount of time, and I feel compelled to tell you about it. Sometimes my opinions find their way in there, but hopefully they aren't overshadowing the main truth in this book: *You are a child of God, and nothing is more important than that.* You won't find perfection here, but you will find some life lessons from the Lord that have helped me grow into a better person.

My book takes place over a six-year span, from 2012 to 2018. God's work in me has been slow but thorough over those six years. I am a completely different person than the girl I was in 2012. Looking back over all that has happened and how it's shaped me into who I am today, I'm filled with so much gratitude for the past and hope for the future. For there is always hope when you're walking hand in hand with Jesus.

In 2012, I was a twenty-six-year-old newlywed who had just quit a job I loved to move across the country with my Air Force husband. It was a huge transition for me. I was born and raised in North Carolina, and I'd lived in Florida for the previous seven years. I'd only moved a few times in my whole life, and now I was joining that whirlwind military life, poised to move every three years for the foreseeable future. This was a turning point for me, a fork in the road, where I could embrace this new life or cross my arms, stick out my bottom lip, and live in a constant pity party because of losing my career and moving to a three-stoplight town in the middle of the desert.

Praise God that He rescued me from that pity party. I didn't choose Him. He chose me. He called me back to Him. He changed my life. A pastor at my church recently said that the Hebrew word for "rescue" doesn't mean lifting you out of a difficult situation. It means something closer to helping us get through the situation and helping us endure it. That's what God did for me, and I think that's what He does for a lot of people.

Throughout this book, I share stories of lessons I learned from the Lord. Some of them are painful lessons I'd rather not repeat. Others are joy-filled, encouraging lessons that I love to share as often as possible, to bring glory to the Lord for all His blessings in my life.

I hope some of you find this book inspirational and encouraging on the road to becoming the mother God wants you to be. Motherhood is not easy. It will bring you to your knees, but God will pick you back up again. He has picked me up more than once, in many different ways. I hope this will encourage you to run to Him for strength and support as I did, when I had three kids under the age of five and my husband was gone for months and the baby pooped in the tub for the third time in a week.

I hope some of you find this book helpful in your journey to becoming a more godly wife. God lays out some pretty specific guidelines for being a wife, and we need to take a close look at those guidelines if we want to live up to the wife He wants us to be. The best part? If you're obedient to the Lord as a wife, your marriage will be blessed many times over.

Brace yourselves. We're going to talk about the big no-no word in today's culture: submission. I promise that if you give it a chance as God intended, you'll stop being turned off by this word. I'm not going to turn you into a doormat who obediently does her husband's bidding at all times! I do think it's worth taking a closer look at how God designed marriages to function. Don't skip that part because the idea of being submissive to your husband nauseates you! Give it a chance.

I hope you find encouragement in this book for how to be a better friend and sister in Christ. Christian friendships are critical to our walk with the Lord. It's so much harder to go through life without other women to help us, rebuke us, build us up, and remind us that our worth comes from God, not from anything here on earth. We live in a fast-paced, social-media-crazed world that has made it all too easy to be swayed by worldly views on important issues. That's why it's so important to surround yourself with people who build you up and fill your head and heart with truth from the Lord.

Most of all, I hope this book helps you discover grace and make it ever-present in your life— grace for yourself and grace for others. We live in a fallen world, and none of us is perfect. We desperately need God's grace to overcome our mistakes and forgive others' mistakes. If I had to pick one word I believe God chose for me, it would be "grace." Grace leads to love, kindness, mercy, and forgiveness. When I started focusing on applying it to every aspect of my life, so many things changed for the better.

I believe there's a reason God put this book in your hands right now. Maybe there's something you can glean from what I've experienced in the past six years. God gave you this book to teach you something or prepare you for something. I hope you stop for a moment and say a quick prayer, thanking the Lord for giving you this book and asking Him to make you sensitive to whatever you're supposed to gain by reading this.

Lord, I lift up in prayer each person reading this book. I pray they find something in this book that moves their heart. I pray they listen to that little voice or feeling and tune in to what You are trying to teach them. I pray any inspiration they find is truly from You, and I pray they run with it, not away from it. Lord, I pray each person reading this book passes it on to someone else when they're done. Help this book find its way into the hands of anyone who needs to hear my story. If a person reading this is not yet a believer in Christ, I pray a mustard seed of faith has been planted by my testimony. I pray they seek out a church, seek out some welcoming believers, and learn more about what Jesus did for them. God, keep us all humble and walking in the spirit of Jesus' love. In Your holy name we pray, amen.

Chapter 1

The Path Begins with a Plus Sign

I saw the plus sign on the home pregnancy test, and everything changed. That sounds pretty stereotypical and clichéd, right? A woman's life changes when she sees the results of her first positive pregnancy test. But for me, it was a game-changer. A marriage saver. An eternity saver. Or, perhaps more accurately, a step toward saving my eternal life.

You see, before that little plus sign showed up, things were not going well in my life. My marriage was struggling. I was lonely. I despised my job. I lived across the country from all my friends and family. God was far from my mind, despite it being a time when I needed Him most.

I grew up in a Christian home. I was taught that Jesus is our Savior and died for our sins so we may spend eternity in heaven. I knew all the basic Bible stories. I attended church on Christmas and Easter and occasionally in between. I was taught morals based on biblical values, and I certainly knew what it meant to obey the Lord. But somewhere along the way, God sort of went fuzzy and out of focus in my mind. I knew He was there. I never stopped believing in Him. I never stopped believing in Jesus or what He did for me. But I also never thought about it.

I attended boarding school starting at age thirteen and didn't go back to church for at least a decade. I rarely prayed. I did not live my life for the Lord. I lived my life for me. What felt good for me, what got me the best results, what made people like me the best, that's what I did. That's what governed my life. And that's what led me down the path to that low point in 2012 when I was staring at that positive pregnancy test in the bathroom of our small home in New Mexico.

A few days after learning I was pregnant, God started knocking on my door. It was like a little whisper in my ear: "Hello, Chrissie, I'm still here. I think it's time you come back to Me." I heard it but thought little of it. I did start making changes in my life as I tried to be a better person, but God wasn't my motivation yet. I just knew I was bringing a child into this world and wanted to be the best mommy I could be.

And I wanted to be a better wife so I could set a good example. I wanted to be a better friend and employee and sister and daughter. It was as if that little baby growing in my womb motivated me to try harder to live for others rather than for myself. I think it was the first time I put someone else's needs above my own. Living for that baby became priority number one.

Around this same time, my dad was going through a transformation, beginning to live his life for the Lord, which of course turned him into a completely different person. Almost every aspect of Dad's personality was different, and he just seemed so happy. I knew part of that was his relationship with a wonderful Christian woman who would soon become his wife, but I could tell there was more to it.

Nearly every conversation with him led back to the Lord. He never made a significant decision without going to the Lord in prayer first. And he seemed so confident and sure that the Lord was speaking to him. This fascinated me. I'd never been around someone who was walking with God in this way before, and I didn't know what to make of it. But looking back now, I know God was using my dad to draw me to Him. It seemed that each time I talked to my dad, I grew more and more curious about God. I started praying regularly. I may have cracked open the Bible a time or two. But it was slow progress, not even noticeable to my husband. Admittedly, our marriage was not in a great state at this point, so we weren't noticing much about each other, but I'll explain that later.

After our daughter Kelly was born, I quit my job to stay home with her. I suddenly found myself with a huge amount of free time on my hands. God was giving me an opportunity to slow down and get to know Him, though I didn't recognize it. Once I got past the early baby months of sleepless nights and foggy days, I found myself looking for a way to fill the time. That's when I got my first devotional, courtesy of Dad. *Experiencing God* was the title, and it intimidated me. It was thick and time-consuming, but something drove me to dive right in, and I ate it up.

It taught me how to pray, how to start developing a relationship with God, how to understand scripture, and how to memorize scripture. I quickly fell in love with studying the Bible and speaking to God. But I also felt disappointed when I didn't immediately start hearing from Him. Isn't that how it goes? We want instant results! I'm reading my Bible, I'm praying, I'm memorizing scripture—now where's my direct, all-access line to the man upstairs? Hello?

Thanks to some meaningful conversations with my dad and a few other mature Christians, I was able to get over that frustration and realize a few things. I *did* have a direct all-access line to the Lord. He was always listening, and frequently answering, just not in the way I expected. I wanted to literally hear Him, and when that didn't happen, I thought something was wrong. But the more I read about prayer, the more I realized that hearing from God could be much more than something we do with our ears.

We can hear God when we're having a hard day, and in that moment of desperation, our baby smiles up at us. We can hear God when we pray for relief from the weeks of sleepless nights and wake up the next morning to discover the baby finally slept through the night. We can hear from God when our husbands unexpectedly do the dishes or fold the laundry when we've had a rough day. All the little blessings are God showing us His love.

I continued to develop my relationship with the Lord, but it was slow going. I never had that salvation moment, standing in church, heart racing, ready to throw my hand up when the preacher asks who just believed in Jesus Christ for the first time. If someone asks me when I was saved, my answer usually sounds something like, "Uh, I'm not sure. I've always believed in Jesus but kind of forgot about Him for a while. Then around the time my first daughter was born, I found Him again. Or rather, He found me!" (Insert nervous chuckle.)

I feel as if it's been a slow but steady process over more than five years. And by far, it's the most important thing that's ever happened in my life. It's taken me a while to understand that our eternal salvation is much more important than anything that happens to us on earth. But having my first child certainly took me a step closer to grasping that concept. The love I felt for that child the moment I knew she was in my womb overwhelmed me.

As I slowly got to know the Lord and learned that His love for us is about a gazillion times bigger than my love for my own children, I started to understand why anything He wants is more important than anything I want. He expressed His love for me by giving up His only Son. To save *me*. And He didn't stop there. He loves me, so He continually blesses me and gives me strength to survive this fallen world! The least I can do is respect and obey His commands.

Thankfully, those early days of getting to know the Lord were easy-breezy days full of laughter, play, and peaceful naptimes. Having one child didn't provoke any of those ugly mommy moments that were sure to come in the years ahead, when more children entered the picture. Having one child didn't put any extra stress on my marriage, a marriage that was beginning to heal and flourish after Kelly's birth.

My point is, my life was fairly easy during that first year of growing my relationship with God, so I could focus on learning about Him and His Word and His Son and all that. I wasn't trying to navigate my own issues, and I wasn't constantly filling my prayer time with requests or sobbing pleas for help—which were soon to come! I just wanted to learn.

A lot of the Bible can be pretty confusing, especially if you're trying to understand it on your own. Much of it is so easily taken out of context and made into pretty memes you see on Facebook or Instagram. Without the proper guidance, you can easily misunderstand huge chunks of God's Word.

So the next step in my spiritual growth was to find a church. I believe that if you want to grow as a child of God, you need to surround yourselves with brothers and sisters in Christ, to teach and encourage one another. Though to be honest, in those early stages of my walk, I felt as if I needed to find a church out of obedience. If you want to be close to God, you have to go to church on Sunday, right?

Thankfully, Michael was on board, and we started going to the Baptist church down the street. Michael grew up occasionally attending Baptist churches, and

I had no affinity for any particular denomination, so Bethel Baptist Church seemed as good a choice as any. At the time, it didn't even dawn on me to ask God to lead us to the right church. But our faithful Lord did it anyway. Aren't we fortunate that He answers the prayers we forget to ask?

This little church was a huge answered, though unasked, prayer. The congregation was welcoming, the pastors were kind, and the music was fun. The small groups were interesting, and we got donuts every Sunday! I was a little nervous that Michael wouldn't want to keep up the church-every-Sunday thing. In the past, it took quite a bit of persuasion to get him out the door on a Sunday morning. The Lord hadn't seemed to put that desire in him yet. But never count God out. Our pastor tailored every sermon to whichever big event was in the news that week, which kept Michael interested. He was very into current events at that time. Looking back, I think God put us with that pastor to help keep Michael coming.

It was a great church. If you're ever in Alamogordo, New Mexico, look for Bethel Baptist Church on Scenic Drive, at the base of some beautiful mountains. Our pastor isn't there anymore; he's at a small, rural church in Virginia, which happened to be where we ended up four years later. But that's a story for another day.

In that first devotional I did, the first verse I memorized was John 15:5: *"I am the vine; you are the branches. If a man remains in me and I in him, he will bear much fruit; apart from me you can do nothing."* That's probably the only verse I still remember of the twelve verses I memorized while using that devotional. I'm terrible at memorization! But that verse has never left me. I have remained in God, and He has remained in me. There has been so much fruit. And it all started with that little one growing in my belly.

Chapter 2

Zero Proof, Please

The Lord used two big events in my life to call me to Him in the year I got pregnant with Kelly. The first was the new life in my womb, which I assumed would change everything. *I* certainly was changing, but nothing around me seemed any different. I was still miserable at my job. I was still unhappy in my marriage. I was still questioning pretty much every decision I had made that led me to that point.

I had been a successful television news producer in Tallahassee, the same town where I went to college, surrounded by friends and only a few hours from family. Then Michael got commissioned—meaning he became a commanding officer—in the Air Force, and we moved across the country to his new duty station.

Why did I quit my job, in my career field, in the city with all my friends, to move to a tiny town in the middle of the desert in New Mexico? Why had I given up everything I loved to follow a man? Isn't that the opposite of what we're told women are supposed to do these days? The initial rush of the positive pregnancy test brought me happiness and excitement and a willingness to change. But that started to wear off after a few months, and I was frustrated because I seemed to be the only one changing.

As I said before, don't count God out. I've mentioned our marriage was unhappy, but I haven't gotten into why, because, well, it's not fun to talk about. Especially since we've come so far since then. It's opening old wounds, but I believe God is calling me to speak about it because it brings Him so much glory. So here's the second big event the Lord used to call me to Him.

First, a little backstory: I met Michael when I was nineteen. We both worked at a Ruby Tuesday in Tallahassee and attended Florida State University. My first memory of Michael is from an afternoon shift at the restaurant. I was a hostess, and he was a brand-new waiter. He made a rose out of a napkin and gave it to me, even though we'd just met. A few weeks later, my boyfriend of a year dumped me, and Michael wanted to cheer me up, so he invited me to a party after work. The rest is history, as they say. We officially started dating a few months later and have been together ever since.

Not many women meet their husband at nineteen; I consider myself blessed. And in hindsight, I can see how God worked to keep us together. I mean, *I was nineteen.* Young, dumb, and selfish. Our relationship was a mess. Florida State University is pretty well known for being a party school, and party is exactly what we did. Our life consisted of school, work, and parties.

We had a great time, but we also had a lot of drama. We drank too much, we fought a lot, and we didn't put each other's needs first. We moved in together two and a half years before he even proposed. Ours was not your average sweet Christian romance. We're just two people who somehow survived all the enemy's attempts to split us up.

I now know God was right by our sides the entire time, drawing us back to one another when we'd start to drift apart. He had a bigger plan for us, a plan we couldn't see or imagine in our college days, and I praise Him for never letting us split up. Through all our ups and downs, we knew the love was real. The love was strong enough to weather any mess that we brought upon our-selves. And boy, were we in for a real mess when we got to New Mexico in 2011!

Michael had a drinking problem, but no one realized it until it was almost too late. It started as college drinking and then never slowed down when we left the college scene. It had always been social drinking until we moved to New Mexico. Then it became drinking alone, because we didn't have any friends. The drinking led to fights. So many fights. Ugly, name-calling, heartbreaking fights. And by the summer of 2012, about a month before that pregnancy test came up positive, I was ready to throw in the towel.

I'd grown up with drinking in my family, and I could hardly believe I'd married into drinking. I just wanted to start over. I even told Michael that I was done with him more than once that summer. But then God threw that curveball of a little one growing inside me. And the moment, I mean the *very moment,* I saw that positive test, I knew I had to stay. I had to make it work. We'd just have to figure it out. This was the beginning of me learning to rely on God.

Fast forward to my eighth month of pregnancy. Nothing had changed. I hadn't figured anything out. Michael's drinking had increased, despite my pleas that he slow down because of the baby. It was getting closer and closer to my due date, and every evening I'd watch him drinking heavily, wondering what I would do if I went into labor and he couldn't even drive me to the hospital. I brought this up to him one night, and it seemed to resonate with him a little bit. He agreed to slow down, but that never happened.

And then. Isn't that one of the best parts of a redemption story? The "and then" moment, when God swoops in and rescues us because of His overwhelming, never-ending love? Well, this was my "and then" moment. Michael's "and then" moment. He came home from work and told me to call one of my close friends and ask her to come over. He said he needed to talk to me about something serious, and he wanted her there by my side.

This freaked me out. It was weird. He'd normally never ask me to invite a friend over at a moment's notice, especially right after work when he usually just wanted to relax. My brain was spinning, thinking he was going to tell me he was sick. The word "cancer" was on repeat in my head as I frantically straightened up the house before anyone came over. Isn't it funny how we do that? Even in a moment of impending crisis, I still needed to put the clutter away and fluff the pillows.

He also invited over two of his closest friends. He sat us down in the living room and tearfully said, "I have a drinking problem, and I need help." I will never forget that moment. I was in such shock! He had *never* shown any remorse for his drinking or actions caused by drinking. In fact, whenever I brought up how heavily he was drinking, he would tell me I was making mountains out of molehills or that I was just overreacting because I had grown up with a family member who drank too much.

But now, all of a sudden, he's confessing his problem and asking for help? This was one of the biggest God-moments in my life, watching him be so vulnerable in front of me and our friends in our living room that day. That vulnerability and raw honesty continued over the next several weeks as he talked to the right people who could help him. God moved mountains in Michael's heart that day.

The pivotal moment occurred when his boss was scheduled to read to children during story time at the library that day and Michael accompanied him. As he watched all those little kids listening to the story, he was overcome with emotion, thinking about his own baby on the way and what it would mean to be her father. Michael realized he was in no shape to be a good dad to his baby girl. God touched his heart that day in that library. There's no other explanation for such a huge and instant change of heart. We just didn't know it was God yet.

Michael got help. He got sober. He started attending Alcoholics Anonymous, and I started going to Al-Anon, a program similar to AA but meant for the friends and family members of addicts. Prayer and scripture are a big part of those programs; it helped us grow closer to God and closer to each other. We had a lot of honest conversations and truly began to heal.

Trust was an issue for us at this point, because I hadn't even been aware of the level his drinking had reached. I watched him drink a lot each night, and I would find liquor bottles stashed in random places around the house. But once he came clean about it all, I found out he'd been drinking much more than I had suspected. I felt like a fool. We were living in the same house, and I had no idea what was happening.

The breaking point for all of this was when we started sleeping in different bedrooms. The excuse? I was very pregnant and uncomfortable and needed our entire queen-size bed to myself. So he appeared to be a sweet, accommodating husband who moved into the guest room. This was the key to our undoing, though. I believe a husband and wife should not sleep in separate rooms for an extended period of time. Sleeping apart from each other prompted me to withdraw from him even more, and it allowed him to drink as much as he wanted every night before eventually passing out.

Once I learned how much he'd been hiding from me, I felt I couldn't trust him at all, but our faithful heavenly Father helped restore that trust through a few therapy sessions, a lot of late-night conversations, and prayer.

Did I mention all of this happened about two weeks before Kelly was born? Talk about a whirlwind! Talk about God's incredible timing! In the weeks leading up to Michael's living-room confession, I was sobbing myself to sleep each night, praying for God to show me how to make my marriage work and still keep my baby safe. I was convinced that I was bringing home a baby to a drunken father. How would I protect her? It was getting so close to my due date that I assumed there was no solution other than to figure it out in the moment. I wasn't hearing from God when I prayed, so I assumed my prayers weren't working. And then!

Three kids and almost six years later, Michael is still sober, and our marriage is better than ever. When I think back on my thirty-three years of life and what I'm most grateful for, his sobriety comes close to topping the list. Life changed after he stopped drinking. We fell in love all over again. I stopped drinking too. Not a drop, other than a few sips of champagne at my best friend's wedding in 2014. I know there are marriages that work in which one person is sober and the other isn't. But I felt as if the Lord was telling me to be sober—not just for Michael but also for myself.

When I look back on my drinking days, I realize I didn't make good decisions when I drank. I wasn't a very nice person. That selfish side of me definitely took over when I was drinking. And while I think I could handle a glass of wine here and there just fine, I have no desire to. I want to show solidarity with my husband. I want to always be clear-headed for my children. But I don't judge anyone who chooses to drink. This is the path God led me down. He leads us all down different paths for different reasons. This path works for me and helps me grow closer to becoming the wife and mother God wants me to be.

No temptation has overtaken you except what is common to mankind. And God is faithful; he will not let you be tempted beyond what you can bear. But when you are tempted, he will also provide a way out so that you can endure it (1 Corinthians 10:13).

I'm not going to pretend that it's been smooth sailing, Facebook-perfect, every day since we stopped drinking. It's not always easy to be the only woman abstaining from alcohol during Mommy's Night Out. But it's gotten easier with time—because the Lord sustains me. He doesn't let me be tempted beyond what I can bear. Whenever I'm tempted to drink to join the crowd, He gently reminds me of the alternative, of what my life would be like if I hadn't stopped drinking. If Michael hadn't stopped drinking. And I'll get through a few awkward moments as everyone but me orders a glass of wine any day over the alternative. Though I'm pretty sure a few people assume I'm pregnant whenever this happens.

When tempted, no one should say, "God is tempting me." For God cannot be tempted by evil, nor does he tempt anyone (James 1:13).

We always need to remember where our temptations come from—the enemy. Satan is tricky and persistent and always seems to come for us when we're down. Our biggest fight in this life is not against anything on this earth.

For our struggle is not against flesh and blood, but against the rulers, against the authorities, against the powers of this dark world and against the spiritual forces of evil in the heavenly realms (Ephesians 6:12).

We will always have to fight against forces of evil, even after such a big win from God, like sobriety. But praise God for His armor, His belt of truth, His breastplate of righteousness, His gospel of peace, His shield of faith, His helmet of salvation, and His sword of the Spirit. I pray for God to suit me up in His armor all the time, so I can fight back hard.

When I've had a particularly hard day with the kids and Michael is out of town, the enemy will whisper temptation in my ear: "You should go get some wine. It will help relieve all this stress. Michael isn't even here; he'll never know." Praise the Lord for saving me and changing my heart of stone into a heart of flesh. A heart that respects her husband and puts his needs above her own. A heart that knows how to fight back. Six years ago, I would never have thought that way. The enemy would have won. But not today, Satan!

Chapter 3

When Oceans Rise...

By the time Kelly turned one, things were feeling pretty good. My marriage was in a good place and getting better. The trust had been reestablished. It was as if Michael and I fell in love all over again after he got sober. We'd spent an entire year rediscovering one another, and our marriage blossomed. We even started to get out and about, exploring what turned out to be an interesting part of the country. On Saturdays we'd drive up to a small mountain town nearby or travel a few hours to see some obscure landmark. We went hiking in caverns and even visited a nuclear testing site.

We also got involved in our church, attending small-group classes and volunteering when we could. We were even baptized together, a day I consider more special than our wedding day. Looking into his eyes right before we both went under the water was magical, knowing we were coming back up even stronger, thanks to our salvation and new relationship with Christ. It was a special moment for me personally, because it was a public declaration of my beliefs. I'm not big on doing anything publicly in front of a big group of people, but I couldn't wait to be submerged in that water in front of the congregation. Add in the fact that my husband was doing it *by my side,* and I was thrilled! It felt like a representation of the do-over God had given us with Michael's sobriety.

I also started to feel as if I had a handle on the whole stay-at-home-mom gig. I wasn't bored or lonely. I loved my solo time with baby Kelly. We went on walks, we went to the playground, we took our pup to the dog park. We even had fun at the grocery store. (Ah, how I miss those days with one child in the grocery store, when I had time to laugh and play and explore the produce section with a curious little one. Now every grocery trip feels like a trip through a war zone, and I barely come out alive in the end. But I digress.)

I felt I was on solid ground at this point, for the first time in a while. I could handle a twelve-month-old. I wasn't frantically checking her crib to see if she was breathing anymore. I knew what her various cries meant. I had a handle on most of it, except for her eating habits. Why are one-year-olds so hard to feed? I could cook fifteen different things, and she wouldn't eat any of them! This might be OK for those chubby babies out there, but my skinny minny had me worried! Anyway, I digress again…it's my #mombrain. My walk with the Lord was there. But it was in its early stages and fairly immature. I prayed nightly but rarely thought to speak to God throughout the day. I seldom opened the Bible for guidance, but I was reading it during an almost-daily devotional time. I was growing but slowly. Nothing was going on in my life that forced me to desperately seek the Lord. There was no real hardship.

Until I got a call from Michael one morning. His orders had finally come in. The Air Force was moving us to Guam. Guam! I had to Google it to find out where on earth that tiny island was. And I was pumped! What an adventure! I felt nothing but excitement and happiness in those first few moments of hearing we were headed halfway around the world in a few months.

But that excitement quickly turned to trepidation when I started thinking about the logistics of moving that far away with a baby, two pets, two cars, and a house full of stuff. Not to mention the fact that moving across the *country* had been hard for me; how on earth was I going to handle moving around the world? The unknown seemed so oppressive. Logistics are always what get me down and crush my initial excitement about something new. It's so hard for me to just accept the fact that I don't have to have all the answers to every question right away. I'm impatient when it comes to logistics. And God knows that, so He was ready to use this situation to help me give up some control and trust Him.

The first verse he brought to me in this situation was Philippians 4:8:

"Finally, brothers and sisters, whatever is true, whatever is noble, whatever is right, whatever is pure, whatever is lovely, whatever is admirable—if anything is excellent or praiseworthy—think about such things."

This was the first verse that ever showed up repeatedly in my life over a short period of time. You know what I mean—when you can't deny that God is wanting you to focus on a verse because it shows up in your daily reading and then your friend texts it to you and then it shows up in your Facebook feed, all on the same day. It seemed as if God wanted me to home in on this verse and think about all those good things I felt when Michael first told me we were moving to Guam. The true things, the lovely things, the praiseworthy things. Not the negative stuff or the worries. (It might have been even more helpful to go back a couple of verses and see what God wanted us to do about our worries, but I wasn't quite there yet.) And to be honest, I didn't realize any of this stuff until much later on.

I knew God was bringing that verse to me for a reason, thanks to the wise counsel of more mature Christians, but I didn't know why. I didn't connect it to my impending move around the world. And it would have been oh-so-helpful if I had been able to find comfort in it at the time, but God was growing me in His own time. (If I ever find the courage to get a tattoo, it will most likely have something to do with Philippians 4:8. There's something so special about the first verse God uses to get your attention.)

Even though I couldn't yet make the connection between Philippians 4:8 and my move, God was still giving me other little pieces of comfort through His Word. One day my Bible reading brought me to Psalm 139:9-10:

"If I rise on the wings of the dawn, if I settle on the far side of the sea, even there your hand will guide me, your right hand will hold me fast."

I felt as if He was specifically telling me that He would be with me the entire way "across the sea." That started to develop this sense of trust. I admit that was a hard one for me in the beginning of my walk, trusting something so intangible. I think it's easier for me now because I have all the evidence of the ways God has worked in my life and the lives of those around me. But when I was a baby Christian, I felt I had no proof of His works, and I struggled with blind trust.

I didn't doubt His existence or the significance of Jesus' death on the cross, but I guess I doubted that God was going to help me through the day-to-day struggles of life. They seemed too insignificant. I felt that was something I was responsible for and needed to control. The idea of giving up control of my life was difficult for me. But if there's ever a time to trust God with your life, it's when you're boarding a plane with an eighteen-month-old to fly for thirty-six hours to a different part of the world, knowing you're about to stay there for three years. Did I mention I was also six months pregnant with baby number two?

That move halfway around the world was a humbling experience for me. I went from thinking it was my job to control my life to realizing it was impossible for me to control my life or do this thing alone. I needed God to get me through this huge transition. If I thought life with a newborn was tough, how was I possibly going to handle life with a newborn and a toddler? In a new country? With no friends and nothing familiar? Sure, I put a smile on my face and told everyone how excited I was about all the upcoming changes and made myself sound very brave and resilient. Because that's what we do, right? We feel this compulsion to always share the positive and hide the negative. And there's something to be said for trying to not be a Debbie Downer all the time!

But it's hard to glorify God and the amazing things He does in your life if you don't share the darkness that comes before the dawn. I was scared. Scared of a new and unfamiliar home, scared of how Michael's job had him traveling a lot, scared of making new friends, scared of adding another little one to the family for me to take care of. I found myself in prayer more often, and it comforted me. There's something about talking to our heavenly Father that soothes my soul. It fills me with peace. At least, it did at that time. I wasn't looking for answers or desperately waiting to hear His voice anymore. I just wanted someone to listen to my worries and complaints. He was a good sounding board for me during that time of uncertainty. I hadn't yet learned how to listen to Him or the importance of listening to Him, but in those early days of my walk, I was certain He was listening to me, and that was enough.

So here I was, living in this tropical paradise, baby number two's arrival just a couple of months away, and I was feeling pretty good. The physical move was scary and forced me to look to the Lord for courage and strength, but things settled down once we found a house and started to familiarize ourselves with the island. Then I started to lose sight of God again. Looking back, that shows me how immature my walk was. I only looked to God in times of trouble. I guess I hadn't come across 1 Thessalonians 5:16-18 yet:

"Rejoice always, pray without ceasing, give thanks in all circumstances; for this is the will of God in Christ Jesus for you."

And you know what happened? Things started to take a turn for the worse.

Michael and I started fighting again. I was pregnant and hot all the time and lonely and taking care of a toddler and all the things that make someone less than desirable to be around. Plus, we didn't have a church home yet.

We hadn't even started looking for a church. I think that was a big part of our problem in those first few months in Guam. There's something about having a church to call home that helps keep other things in place.

It's a nice refresher every Sunday, when you get to worship the Lord in song and then listen to a meaningful
lesson from the pastor. But a true church home provides
so much more than corporate worship once a week. You
meet like-minded people who hold you accountable.
This walk isn't easy, and we need brothers and sisters in
Christ to encourage us. Harvest Baptist Church brought
us all those things we lacked.

Once we started regularly attending HBC and getting
involved with the congregation, things started to look
up again. It was a step of obedience, and I believe God
blessed us for that step. I learned so much in that church.
It was the first time I felt part of a family in a church
setting. That congregation was so kind to us, right from
the beginning. The pastor's wife even gave me a baby
gift when she'd only known me a few weeks! I think
part of that hospitality comes from everyone being so
far away from their own family; they start to view each
other as a real family. And I think it's also part of the culture of Guam, where family is such a central focus. But
most importantly, I think God was showing Michael and
me the importance of church and how it can be so much
more than a weekly meeting place where you sing a little
and listen to sermons. Harvest Baptist Church taught
us what to look for in future churches—how to find a
church that truly feels like home.

For where two or three are gathered in my name, there am I with them (Matthew 18:20).

Where there is no guidance, a people falls, but in an abundance of counselors there is safety (Proverbs 11:14).

Chapter 4

Soul Improvement

Our second child, Clayton, was born at the end of January in 2015, just three short months after we moved across the globe. Mercifully, my mother-in-law was able to fly all the way to Guam to help out with the ridiculousness of bringing home a newborn with a one-year-old at home too. I don't think we would have survived those first few weeks with two kids if it hadn't been for Nana. We believe God sent her to us because He knew we couldn't do it without her.

But eventually she had to go home, and we started to adjust to being a family of four. Within a few months, we had a good system in place, and life was rolling along pretty smoothly. We figured out how to tag-team everything. There were two of us and two children, so we each took a child during the chaotic times, like dinner and bedtime. I'd even settled into a good rhythm during the day when Michael was at work. I didn't accomplish much during those early days with two small kiddos at home, but we all survived.

Remember how I said at this point in my walk, I rarely turned to God when things were good? Well, I guess He was ready to teach me a lesson. Clayton had just turned four months old when Michael came home from work, sat me down in the kitchen, and told me he was deploying to Kuwait for four months. Oh, and he was leaving in ten days. (For those of you unfamiliar with military life, you usually get a much longer notice before a deployment. Like, months of notice. On the other hand, there are also many deployments that last a lot longer than four months, so beggars can't be choosers, I suppose.) To say I was distraught would be quite the understatement.

We had just figured out this whole toddler-and-a-baby thing! Now I have to do it alone? In Guam, with no family to help? I had made a few friends at this point, but no one was close enough to be called on to help in a real way, with day-to-day life. God was ready to bring me to my knees so I would learn what it meant to trust Him and rely on Him for every little thing.

We soaked up those last ten days with Michael, and then I waved a tearful goodbye at 4 a.m. on the day he left. My world had turned upside down. My son was the worst sleeper as a baby, and I don't handle lack of sleep very well. I certainly wasn't winning any Mother of the Year awards during that time. I was in survival mode, barely getting through the day. I yelled too much at my two-year-old and, let's be honest, I probably yelled at the baby, too. I was sleep deprived, alone, and quickly losing my mind.

Nothing will bring you to your knees quicker than seeing your sweet little girl's eyes filled with terror because you just screamed at her like a psychopath for not putting her shoes on fast enough. I remember that day so clearly. I knew in that moment that my only recourse was to go to God and beg for help. I shut both crying kids in their rooms and went to my bedside. I got down on my knees, sobbing, and begged the Lord to show me how to change, how to be kinder to my children, how to just *stop yelling all the time*.

That was the first step in changing my ways that summer. I finally turned to God for help. He showed me that what I was doing was not OK, and He showed me that He was the answer. But somehow, I missed that second part. So, first I looked for a worldly answer to my problems. I found a great group of moms on Facebook who were trying to stop yelling. They had all sorts of ideas on ways to change this habit. I created an entire notebook devoted to being a calmer mommy. I plastered my kitchen and bathrooms and door frames with encouraging sayings and reminders. I followed their recommended system, and it worked, for a little while.

But before long, I was right back to screaming at my kids again, and I felt even worse than before I'd started the whole thing. I knew nothing of giving myself grace. I knew nothing about all the scripture verses that provide answers on how to be a kind and gentle person. I'd looked everywhere but the Bible for ways to live my life, and it wasn't working. (I want to take a minute to say that I'm not trying to discount the nonbiblical methods for fixing whatever your issue is, whether it's yelling at your kids or something else entirely. But I learned from experience that using those methods alone, without tying them to biblical principles, just won't work in the long run.)

I can't remember what changed my mind and got me started with devotionals during naptime again, as I'd done when Kelly was a baby. All I can say is that God was moving in my heart. I stopped studying the social media pages for information about how to be a gentle mother, and I started studying the Bible during my free time. I began reading Mark Batterson's *Draw the Circle* devotional, and it changed my prayer life. In his book,

Batterson talks about walking in a circle around your home or business or church or whatever you're praying about and praying while you walk in that circle. So I walked around the outside of my home every day, praying for peace in my heart, peace in all the rooms, peace, peace, peace. It was as if I craved it, like my body and soul knew it was seriously lacking. Sometimes I walked that circle holding a crying Clayton in my arms. Sometimes I walked that circle in the rain. But I did it over and over and over again until I felt as if I was finally starting to feel some peace.

That devotional brought me too many amazing lessons to count, but two big ones stand out in my memory. The first was to do the little things as if they are big things. This was so applicable to my life in that season. It seemed all I was doing was little stuff. Changing diapers, making meals, washing clothes, cleaning bathrooms. I had no life outside of motherhood. But God showed me that motherhood *is* a big thing. All that little stuff adds up to big stuff! Everything I say and do as a mom will shape the kind of person my kids grow up to be. (*No pressure, right?*) Every day I was planting tiny seeds in my kids, seeds that will affect my grandkids and great-grandkids. Can you get much bigger than that? The Lord helped me find some worth in my daily life as a mom, and that helped me regain some control over my actions.

The second lesson was all about God's timing. I wanted to be a better, gentler mom who never yelled at her kids, and I wanted that *now*. I felt that because I hadn't changed my ways in just a few days, I was a failure. I never stopped to look back at how slowly God had moved some of the mountains in my life. His timing is perfect, and while we may never understand it, we can always trust it.

Wanting instant results has always been a problem for me. I rarely stick to a diet or workout routine, because I don't have the patience to wait to see the fruit of my labor. That attitude sets us up for failure as a parent. We won't see the fruits of our labor for *years*, if at all. What a big game of trust—that we're doing the right thing, making the right decisions, and aren't ruining our children.

I'm writing this three and a half years after I read the *Draw the Circle* devotional, and I still struggle to be that gentle mother to my kids. But looking back, I can see a lot of progress, a lot of proof that God is answering my prayers and working on me. The lesson of trusting in His timing was a big one not only in motherhood but in just about every other thing I've wanted in my life.

I'm not going to pretend like this devotional brought about some permanent fix, and I'm now this lovely, peaceful, soft-spoken mother who never loses her cool. Far from it! I've regressed so many times, it's not even funny. In fact, I probably need to go walk some circles around my house right now. But that summer, when I was so alone and so desperate for help, God was the only place for me to turn, and He taught me the value of growing a close relationship with Him. I may have still yelled at my kids here and there, but because I was studying His Word, I learned to give myself grace, not expect perfection, and know that He still loves me when I mess it all up. That right there was enough to ease the tension and stress in my home and bring us some peace. Once I stopped beating myself up about it all the time, I found myself yelling less. My overall stress was lessened, and we became a much happier home.

My other fear during Michael's deployment was that our marriage would suffer after being apart for so long. We had just overcome some big obstacles, and I was so worried that we'd be back to square one when he got home. When I finished the *Draw the Circle* devotional, I looked for something on marriage and how to be a godly wife. Y'all, I cannot praise *The Respect Dare* enough. It should be a mandatory devotional for women before they get married. I spent every afternoon diving into this devotional and learning about the kind of wife God designed us to be.

I'll be honest—it's a hard pill to swallow at first. It goes against almost everything current society teaches us about how to be a successful woman. I felt I had to unlearn everything I'd been taught about the kind of woman I'm supposed to be in this day and age. I mean, the word "submit" appeared a lot in the pages of that book, and that's a word we aren't all that comfortable with these days. But I learned what God meant by "*submit*." The word doesn't mean you become a doormat who does your husband's bidding at all times. It takes a strong woman to know when to speak up and voice her opinion, and when to keep quiet and let her husband lead the way. After all, God appointed husbands to be the spiritual leader of the family. We need to let them lead.

If your husband is not fulfilling his role as the spiritual leader of the family, that can certainly make things more difficult. My advice to you is to pray for the Lord to speak to your husband's heart and guide him toward that leadership role. Not all men are natural-born leaders, but they're all called to lead their own families. If you stay faithful and trust the Lord to do a good work in your husband, he will eventually become the leader he's meant to be.

I also learned how to be respectful of my husband. God designed men to crave that respect from their wives. It means more than almost anything else to them. That was a real lightbulb moment for me. I hadn't been intentionally disrespectful to Michael, but I wasn't showing him the kind of respect God wants wives to show their husbands. I wasn't letting him be the leader of our family. I wasn't giving his decisions and opinions the importance they deserved. I was trying to make myself equal or above him in the family hierarchy, and it wasn't working—because that's not how God designed marriages to work! But nearly every movie and sitcom from the last twenty-plus years shows the wife being the head of the family, making all the decisions, and the husband is like some kind of puppet who's expected to do whatever it takes to make his wife happy. This is not how God wants our marriage to work. I'm not sure where this concept came from, but we need to be countercultural in our marriages if we want them to succeed. Respect your husband and let him act in the way God created him to act.

One of my biggest lessons from this devotional was applying James 1:19 to my life:

"This you know, my beloved brethren, but everyone must be quick to hear, slow to speak and slow to anger."

I can blame it on lack of sleep from babies and postpartum hormones, but I've always been hot-tempered and talked too much in the wrong moments. I knew that changing this about myself could make a huge difference in my marriage. It would show Michael so much respect if I would just pause in a heated moment, listen to what he has to say, and then respond with grace and kindness. Of course, my first thought was that I wanted *him* to do all that for *me*. But I felt an assurance that if I could change this about myself, he would follow suit. And *he did*! It was such a game-changer for us and a lesson in how God's blessings start to show up when we're being obedient to His Word. I even pushed harder and tried to apply this lesson outside my marriage—in my friendships, in motherhood. I felt changes happening all around me, in the best way.

I also learned a lot about myself as I read about how to be a better wife. One of my biggest flaws? I complain about *everything*. Or at least, I used to. Philippians 2:14 says,

"Do everything without grumbling or arguing."

And the Proverbs 31 wife is

"clothed with strength and dignity; she can laugh at the days to come."

If she can laugh at the days to come, I'm thinking that means she isn't bogged down by her daily life, complaining about how much housework she has or how the kids never listen to her.

God convicted me about my complaining nature as I examined how to be a better wife to Michael. Through that devotional, He showed me how much I complain about the little stuff throughout the day. How can I expect my husband to have a good attitude when he gets home from work if he's always greeted by a sour-faced wife who's got a laundry list of things that went wrong all day? There's a time and place to vent our frustrations to our husbands, but if 90 percent of our dialogue involves complaining about our lives, it results in too much negativity.

God wants us to think about

"whatever is true, whatever is noble, whatever is right, whatever is pure, whatever is lovely, whatever is admirable" (Philippians 4:8—there's that verse again!).

If we respect our husbands as a gift from God, we will focus on those positive things so we can help him focus on those as well.

Wives, submit yourselves to your own husbands as you do to the Lord. For the husband is the head of the wife as Christ is the head of the church, his body, of which he is the Savior. Now as the church submits to Christ, so also wives should submit to their husbands in everything. Husbands, love your wives, just as Christ loved the church and gave himself up for her to make her holy, cleansing her by the washing with water through the word, and to present her to himself as a radiant church, without stain or wrinkle or any other blemish, but holy and blameless. In this same way, husbands ought to love their wives as their own bodies. He who loves his wife loves himself. After all, no one ever hated their own body, but they feed and care for their body, just as Christ does the church—for we are members of his body. "For this reason a man will leave his father and mother and be united to his wife, and the two will become one flesh." This is a profound mystery—but I am talking about Christ and the church. However, each one of you also must love his wife as he loves himself, and the wife must respect her husband. (Ephesians 5:22-33).

It says it right there in Ephesians. First, Paul talks about the wife submitting to her husband, just as the church submits to Jesus. Then he talks about husbands loving their wives, almost as if that comes *as a result of* the wife submitting or showing respect. I know Michael loved me even before I was working hard to be a respectful wife. But that love grew so much after I started being obedient to God in His role for me as a wife. Obedience brings blessings from the Lord, and my marriage has certainly been blessed!

Don't be afraid of the words "submit" or "respect." They don't have to be scary concepts, even for millennial women. It's countercultural, sure. But isn't everything about Jesus countercultural? I've almost reached the point where I'm excited to do something countercultural. Our current culture leaves much to be desired.

I believe you can be a submissive and respectful wife and a strong woman at the same time. I think it's an especially important thing to strive for if you are a mother to daughters. I want to be a good example for my daughters of how to be the kind of wife God wants us to be while still being a strong woman. A good husband is supposed to be the leader of the family, but he should still value his wife's opinion. I think if we give our opinion in a respectful way, rather than a bossy or nagging way, it's more likely to be well-received.

Another aspect of a good wife is not withholding your body from him. I'm not going to spend too much time talking about sex, but I'd be remiss if I didn't at least mention it as part of my path to becoming a better wife. Concerning the marital bed, the Bible says,

"Do not deprive each other except perhaps by mutual consent and for the time, so that you may devote yourselves to prayer. Then come together again so that Satan will not tempt you because of your lack of self-control" (1 Corinthians 7:5).

It's so easy to push your husband away at bedtime when you're exhausted from twelve hours with needy toddlers or a hard day at work. It may not seem like that big of a deal to keep putting it off, but sex is a gift from the Lord for married couples. And He commands us to not deprive one another of that gift.

When I decided I wanted to change my attitude about sex, I was afraid it would start to feel like an obligation, since I was just trying to make sure I didn't deprive him. But God is so good and full of blessings. When I made a conscious effort to stop pushing Michael away all the time, God changed my heart toward sex. It didn't feel like an obligation at all. It became something I enjoyed and looked forward to, no matter how tired I was. Of course, I still have days when the exhaustion overwhelms me, and I have to ask for a raincheck. So does he! But those days are much easier to handle when they are the exception, not the norm.

I soaked up everything about how to be a biblical wife from *The Respect Dare*, and I couldn't wait to apply all of it to our marriage once Michael returned. It was a real turning point for us, and I believe it saved our marriage almost as much as his sobriety did. It seemed as if it changed the overall tone of our relationship when I changed my actions and reactions to him. He was starting to get that respect he craved, and in turn, was starting to be much more helpful and accommodating to me. It's as if we slowly fixed all the broken pieces.

As with my yelling-at-the-kids problem, I'm not going to pretend things have been perfect in my marriage since I learned how to be a respectful wife. Sometimes I mess it all up, my flesh gets the best of me, and I don't care about showing him any respect in a tough moment. And I promise you, that moment is always worse when I choose to honor my own pride over his need for respect.

Or we have moments when I do show respect, even though I may not want to, but Michael's flesh gets the best of him, and he doesn't receive it in a loving way. We're human: we mess up all the time. But I can say without a shadow of a doubt that working toward being a godly wife will change your marriage for the better, and the love between you and your husband will grow in amazing ways. If all else fails, just follow this blueprint:

Love is patient and kind; love does not envy or boast; it is not arrogant or rude. It does not insist on its own way; it is not irritable or resentful; it does not rejoice at wrongdoing but rejoices with the truth. Love bears all things, believes all things. Love never ends (1 Corinthians 13:4-8).

Chapter 5

Into the Deep

One of the cool things about living in Guam is how accessible and affordable it is to become a certified scuba diver—something I had no desire to do, but Michael was dying to try it. When we first got to the island, I told him there was no way he was going to get me to dive. He might as well give up on the dream of a husband and wife diving duo and go find a buddy to dive with. He accepted this from me, probably wasn't surprised by it, and never brought it up again.

While he was deployed that first year in Guam, I went through several devotionals and started growing closer to the Lord. One of those devotionals challenged its readers to find a way to prove you trust God, and scuba diving popped into my head. I still had no desire to do it, but I knew I'd be doing something for my husband. It would give us an outside-the-box date activity and most importantly, would show that I trusted God to protect me under water, give me the strength to get through the certification classes, and sustain me in this attempt to do something nice for Michael. When Michael got home from his deployment, I surprised him with this newfound confidence to dive. He was all for it.

In case you've never gone through a dive certification class, let me tell you a little something about it. It's awful. Diving in general is wonderful, but the classes stink. They have to prepare you for every bad scenario under water, so you know how to react and don't panic and drown. Mine was a three-day class, starting in a swimming pool on the first day. Guam is a hot island; it's near the equator and has high temperatures in the 80s year-round. But for some reason, on the first day of our certification classes, it had rained all day and was freezing in that pool at 5 p.m. when we jumped in. Not the best start to something I didn't want to do in the first place. I spent the entire day vigorously applying essential oils in hopes that they'd boost my courage and stop the uncomfortable knots in my stomach. Eventually the time came to take our first breath under water, and I'll admit, that was pretty cool. But then. The instructors wanted us to take our masks off and put them back on under water. I realize this sounds pretty simple, but it wasn't.

When you're wearing the mask, it covers your nose. As soon as you take it off, you have to think hard about not breathing through your nose. Apparently, my brain struggles with this, and it took me more than one attempt to master this skill. At one point, I panicked and tried to kick to the surface, but my instructor grabbed me and held me down until I calmed down and figured out how to get the mask back on while staying under water. Did I mention that I've never been comfortable in deep water? I can swim just fine, but I'm certainly not winning any races. I love the pool and the beach, but deep water has always kind of freaked me out. So why on earth am I trying to scuba dive? Because I wanted to prove my trust in the Lord in a tangible way. (I also wanted to be a cool wife who did something fun for her husband even though she didn't want to do it.)

I finished that first evening in the pool and did not feel any better about this decision to dive, despite eventually mastering all the skills. I was cold and wet, and there's not much to see at the bottom of a pool anyway. Nothing happened to get me jazzed about this whole thing, so I didn't start day two in the best of moods.

The second day of class was in the ocean, or harbor, and we were going down to thirty feet. I was a basket case. I was too nervous to eat breakfast, so that contributed to the shakiness I felt in my entire body. We listened to our instructors explain what the day was going to be like before suiting up and walking into the water. And that's when I started feeling a panic attack coming on. I pulled Michael aside and told him I didn't think I could do it. I was starting to hyperventilate and couldn't stop shaking. I was pretty sure I was about to puke. Backing out seemed like the best idea. Besides, it wasn't as if the world was going to end if I changed my mind and stayed safely on dry land. So I couldn't hack it. Who cares? Michael has plenty of buddies he can dive with, and we'll find something else to do together as husband and wife. That's what was running through my head as I tried to justify my sudden gigantic need to quit.

You may be wondering why I wasn't praying for God to help me out a little bit. Wasn't I doing this whole thing to prove that God is the one who will help me and sustain me and all that? Well, I told you my relationship with the Lord grew *slowly*. So while, yes, I was ready to give Him all the credit when I finished this thing, I forgot to pray during the process and ask for a little help. Thankfully, God still answers those unasked prayers!

He sent me help in the form of Michael, my sweet and patient husband, who talked me down from my panic attack and managed to convince me to keep going. I have no memory of what he said or did that got me back in that water, but it worked. I think that's one of the most amazing and loving things that God does for His children—He sends us the exact kind of help we need at the moment we need it, <u>even when we don't ask Him for it!</u> The Bible says to go to God in prayer about everything, so I'm assuming He'd prefer that we remember to ask for His help. But how great is it that He loves us *so much*, He'll help us anyway, even when we forget.

I was able to complete day two and day three under water, and I finished the last day of class in love with diving. There is something about being under water and seeing all that sea life up close, while being able to breathe the entire time, that is simply amazing. It makes the whole process seem completely worth it. Plus, day three didn't involve any crazy tasks; we were just diving. When we finished that third day, I surprised Michael by telling him I wanted to get an advanced diver certification as soon as possible. In just three days, I went from being terrified of diving to wanting to do it as much as possible. God gave me so much boldness that I was ready to dive to a hundred feet or swim through a shipwreck! I still felt and continue to feel some trepidation before each dive, but once I'm under water, I'm at ease and feel such a sense of peace. Except for that one time we were on vacation in Australia and Michael and I saw a huge shark swimming right at us. But that's a whole other story.

Unfortunately, we haven't been able to dive since we left Guam in 2017. So I'm kind of back to square one with my nerves about the whole thing. I keep having moments when I tell myself it's fine if I never dive again. I did it for a while, and it was fun, but I can be perfectly content up here on dry land. Then I remember that God didn't send us here to be comfy and cozy our whole lives.

It may sound silly to say that God wants us to leave our comfort zones and go scuba diving, but I think it's a metaphor, or maybe a preparation, for so many other aspects of living a Christian life. If we never leave our comfort zone, how will we spread the gospel and evangelize people not like ourselves? If we never leave our comfort zones, how will we help the least of these? If we never leave our comfort zones, how will we find other sisters and brothers in Christ to help us on our walk? I think God pushed me to dive so I would learn a valuable lesson—I can leave my comfort zone and survive! God will be with me every step of the way, even if I forget to call on Him in my moment of need. He'll swoop in with my magical husband who knows just what to say to keep me moving forward.

It is the Lord who goes before you. He will be with you; he will not leave you or forsake you. Do not fear or be dismayed (Deuteronomy 31:8).

Chapter 6

Purpose Takes the Wheel

A round the same time I was learning to dive, God began to nudge me toward what I now believe is His purpose for my life. I think if you listen closely, God will always tell you why He's put you on this earth. But He'll do it on His own time, which may not be all that convenient for you.

I spent most of my childhood envisioning myself as a professional ballerina, and my family put a lot of time, money, and effort into making that happen. I danced after school, I went to intensive summer ballet programs all around the country, and I went to an art school for high school, a *boarding* art school. I was serious about it.

But after my first year in college, I realized that it wasn't a realistic dream for me, and I switched gears to pursue a media degree, heading straight into the world of television news shortly before I graduated.

Fast forward about seven years, and TV news no longer felt like the right fit either. Some of that may have been due to the fact that I spent the three or four years living in a place that did not have a local television station. I became a stay-at-home mom and felt fairly fulfilled doing that. I loved being home with my kids, taking care of the house, and having time to work on myself. But in November of 2015, God had a new plan for me.

Our church in Guam participated in Orphan Sunday every November. Orphan Sunday is a worldwide initiative to bring awareness to God's call for us to care for orphans. Churches all over the globe dedicate the second Sunday in November solely to this cause, preaching on the different Bible verses that talk about caring for orphans, raising awareness for the need for foster families or people to rally around foster families, and just generally tugging at your heartstrings until you understand this great need in our world. That Orphan Sunday in 2015 changed my life.

I'll admit that prior to that day, I'd never given a passing thought to orphans. I don't mean to sound callous; it just wasn't on my radar and wasn't something I'd ever encountered. But that day, sitting in that pew, listening to the sermon, watching a video about the local foster community on Guam, and hearing how huge the needs are, my heart broke. It was as if the Holy Spirit whispered in my ear, "This is all for you. Open your eyes. Open your heart. This is what you're meant to do." I had no idea what exactly I was supposed to do in relation to the foster community, but I knew it was my calling.

I didn't immediately rush home and start filing paperwork to become a foster parent. Neither Michael nor I felt as if God was telling us to bring a foster child into our home. So I started in the next best place—helping the families who were bringing foster children into their homes. Harvest House is a nonprofit organization on Guam that is dedicated to supporting and serving all the foster families on the island. It was started by a woman named Bethany Taylor when she and her husband took in their first foster child. They realized how many things they had to get when they received the call saying there was a child who needed a home right away. Clothing, shoes, furniture, car seat, crib, formula, diapers, wipes, and so much more. Agreeing to be a foster parent doesn't mean you magically get the funds for everything that comes with it.

Taylor started Harvest House as a place that accepts new and gently used donations of anything a child of any age might need—clothing, toys, toiletries, baby items, books, and so forth. And Harvest House grew and grew. Now it's much more than a closet full of donated items. It's a nonprofit that offers support groups for foster parents, classes for potential foster parents, and several annual events to bring foster families together.

That's where I got my start in the world of orphans. I started volunteering a few times a week, sorting and organizing donations. Within a few months, I knew this was my passion, and I asked for more responsibility. I loved helping those kids. It was magical to see their faces light up when they came in for new clothes or toys, and we had what they wanted. I loved being a part of something that emphasized sharing the gospel with these families as well. The Lord had given me a purpose and put me in a place that also cherished Him and showed gratitude for His many blessings.

I think sometimes the Lord wants us out in the secular world to be the light and spread the gospel. But I also think He knew that at that point in my walk, I would grow more and be better prepared for the future if I was surrounded by believers who held me accountable.

I was so sad to leave Harvest House when we moved away from Guam a couple of years later. I learned so much about having a servant's heart and putting others' needs way above my own. I met some amazing people who said "yes" and inconvenienced their own lives to help a child or, in many cases, multiple children. My eyes were opened to the extreme needs in the foster community.

Of course, a lot more families are needed who are willing to take children into their homes. But they also have a huge need for a bigger and better support system. These families need people to bring them meals from time to time. They need prayer warriors to come along-side them and pray for them. They need childcare for everything from court dates and visitation to date nights so they can recharge their batteries. It's amazing how much you can do to help the foster community even if you can't take children into your own home. Harvest House taught me about all of this, as God used that experience to prepare me for another season.

We left Guam and, after living in Virginia for a year, I found myself in the Florida panhandle, where I still felt that tug to help the foster community. Before our move, I prayed almost daily for God to bring me an opportunity to serve again once we moved to Florida. I'd had my third baby by then, and she was old enough for me to get back into volunteering.

Within two weeks of being in Florida, a local mom posted in a Facebook group that she was looking for donations for a foster closet that was just getting started and was hoping to collect items to give to local foster kids in need. Two weeks. That's all it took for this opportunity to fall into my lap. God is good, y'all. It almost happened faster than I wanted it to. We hadn't even unpacked our belongings! But as I said, God's timing is rarely convenient for us. I immediately messaged her and told her about my experience with Harvest House and how I'd love to join their efforts.

How exciting to be in the beginning phase of something like that! It turned out that the moms who came up with the idea for the foster closet both attended the same church I was joining and had children at the same schools as my kids. Our lives and stories were all different, but we meshed together so seamlessly, and we all brought something different to the table for this project. God had already answered so many prayers as the Gulf Coast Foster Bridge continued to grow. We've added more mothers who feel this calling on their life. And I'm grateful He put me in this place at this time to be a part of it.

Religion that is pure and undefiled before God, the Father, is this: to visit orphans and widows in their affliction, and to keep oneself unstained from the world (James 1:27).

As it's become more and more clear to me that God has called me to help the fatherless, I've become fascinated with how He calls us all to different things. That verse above talks about helping the fatherless *and* the widows. It's a verse I read frequently because it speaks so loudly to me. Yet not once have I thought about helping the widows, and I'm not convinced that's a bad thing. Hear me out before you start thinking I have something against widows. Of course not. I'm just not personally called to help them. If we all try to help everyone, very little will get done. No one will receive any meaningful help. I trust the Lord; therefore, I trust that He's given me the call to help the fatherless, and He's giving someone else the call to help the widows. And someone else the call to help the poor. And someone else the call to help the sick. We are His vessels, and He uses us all to get things done down here.

Last year, a group of my friends was trying to decide on a service project around the holidays. I thought of visiting a children's shelter, but someone else suggested we visit a nursing home. It never would have dawned on me to go to a nursing home. I was so glad she said that, because it reminded me how we all have different callings, and we can all help each other in those different areas. It's easy to get tunnel vision with whatever we're working on, and I do think God calls us to specific causes to devote most of our time and energy to. But it's also good to have brothers and sisters in Christ who can remind us about other needs and make sure we're tending to all God's children.

Right now, I'm fully confident the Lord wants me to focus on helping foster families and foster children and be a part of the support system for them. I am also fully confident that I'm supposed to take a child that is not my own into my home one day. Sometimes I get impatient and want to find that child right now, especially when I hear a tragic story about a child in a bad situation or when I hear the startling statistics about the number of kids in need versus the number of foster families. But I'm learning to listen to God and trust His timing. I'm human, so I still get frustrated and impatient and want to take control sometimes, but I know the only way things will turn out well is if I slow down and wait for God's timing.

Wait for the Lord; be strong, and let your heart take courage; wait for the Lord! (Psalm 27:14).

About a month or two after I started volunteering with the foster closet in Florida, I started feeling that it was time for our family to adopt a child. I woke up thinking about it, I went to bed thinking about it, and it was on my mind all day. I had just read two different books in which the authors had adopted children. It was as if the word "adopt" was written on a giant neon flashing sign hanging in front of my face all day. I felt as if God was trying to tell me it was time. After a couple of weeks, I decided to broach the subject with Michael. We had often talked about adopting one day, even before we had kids of our own, so I was expecting a different response from the one I got.

He was not on board. He wasn't even close. He was only a few months into a new job that was proving to be difficult and frustrating due to things outside his control. His stress level was at like a twelve on a scale from one to ten. He couldn't fathom adding another child to our already busy life. As soon as he told me all this, I understood. The Lord had not put it on his heart. If He had, Michael wouldn't have cared about all that other stuff. I think that's why some families adopt or foster when it seems like the worst time to do it—because God leads them to do it. God clearly was *not* leading Michael to do this. I knew Michael was in tune with the Holy Spirit and would follow that guidance if he sensed it. And I respected Michael as the leader of our family, so I wasn't going to push the idea.

I'd be lying if I said I wasn't disappointed. And confused. I felt *so certain* that God was pushing me down this path to adoption, and then it was as if I hit a brick wall. Why had He put it so heavily on my heart and not put it on Michael's heart at all? It made no sense to me. I tried to find comfort in Isaiah 55:8-9, which says,

> *"'For my thoughts are not your thoughts, neither are your ways my ways,' declares the Lord. 'As the heavens are higher than the earth, so are my ways higher than your ways and my thoughts than your thoughts.'"*

But to be honest, I was frustrated.

A week or two later, the puzzle pieces started to come together. Michael came to me one afternoon and said a large chunk of our credit card debt had been paid off, and he wasn't sure how. At first, we thought we had *finally* been reimbursed by the military for our move from Virginia to Florida, but why would that go to our credit card instead of into our bank account? It didn't make sense. After some digging, Michael finally discovered that all the interest on his credit card bill that had accrued during his many years in the military had been paid off. The credit card company doesn't charge interest for active duty military members, so they had retroactively removed all the interest Michael was incorrectly paying over the years. It was a big chunk of that debt we were trying so hard to pay off. And it happened out of nowhere, without us expecting it at all. What a gift from the Lord! It was a wonderful reminder of how perfect God's timing always is, especially in the middle of my frustration about adoption.

I wasn't trusting God's timing. I was trying to take control. I even had a few moments of anger with God for flashing that adoption sign in my face only to take it away. I lost sight of how a "no" from God might actually be a "not yet." Then He surprised me with an amazing and much-needed financial gift that I hadn't even asked for! It was a real, tangible reminder of how He is always faithful, always keeps His promises, always has our best interest in mind. I still believe God has called my family to adopt a child someday. And now I'm able to trust God with the timing of that.

But they who wait for the Lord shall renew their strength; they shall mount up with wings like eagles; they shall run and not be weary; they shall walk and not faint (Isaiah 40:31).

Chapter 7

Soul Sisters

God always uses our circumstances for something good, and chances are, He will use one situation for multiple things. My time volunteering at Harvest House in Guam prepared me for future opportunities in the same arena, and it expanded my servant's heart, but it also introduced me to one of my favorite people on the planet, Lana, a fellow sister in Christ. How do I describe Lana? She's a tough, no-nonsense girl, whose brain happens to work the way mine does. That is such a rare find! So rare, in fact, that she's the *only* person I've ever met who shares my same way of thinking (other than her ridiculous love for the Clemson Tigers and all things orange). She's a biological mom to three boys and has been a foster mom to many. There aren't many people out there who have three rambunctious boys and still agree to take in more children. Lana's heart is huge.

Lana and I ended up working closely together at Harvest House, and our similar way of viewing the world and taking on projects made for a great partnership. She also felt a calling during that same Orphan Sunday service and immediately started working with Harvest House, beginning with sorting donations as I did, but she eventually ended up running the place—all while taking care of her own three boys and two foster boys. She's basically Wonder Woman. But more importantly for me, God used Lana to show me the importance of having a group of Christian women in similar stages of life that you can turn to in good times and bad.

The idea of having a tribe is trendy right now. Lots of women talk about finding their tribe of females. When you're a Christian, I think it's important to make sure your tribe is made up of Christians. Of course, we are supposed to engage with the world, and that often means interacting with nonbelievers, but I think the people closest to you, the ones you take advice from and tell your secrets to, need to be believers. I never understood the importance of this until I met Lana, and she invited me in to her tribe of Christian sisters.

Lana said she was starting a summer Bible study in her home and wanted to invite me. There were four or five other women, most of whom I knew from church, who already agreed to come. We were kicking things off with a bang, jumping head first into an intense Priscilla Shirer devotional. I admit I was nervous at first. I barely knew these women, and we were supposed to be sharing our innermost desires and fears as we grew together and studied the gospel. But let me tell you, within minutes of that first meeting, I was completely at ease. It was as if the Holy Spirit whisked away all my anxiety and replaced it with peace.

We all cozied up around the living room and began things by sharing our testimonies. That brought a sense of intimacy to the group. I was too nervous to share my complete testimony, so I gave an abridged version, leaving out Michael's drinking and sobriety (*which is a huge part of my testimony*). But as the women shared similar struggles, I realized I could be open with these Christian sisters and never have to fear judgment or gossip. That is one of the best reasons to have a good tribe of Christian women.

Over the next several months, we added some women to our group, and we grew much closer. I found out I was pregnant with number three, and these women were so supportive and helpful, as it wasn't an easy pregnancy.

We did several devotionals together over the next year, and I made some good friends. Almost everyone had a tough moment at some point during that year, tearfully sharing their struggles and asking for prayer. We often laid hands on each other and prayed around the circle.

It was such a time for growth for me, as it was the first time I'd been around women who regularly prayed out loud. I was much too shy to pray aloud. In fact, I don't think I ever prayed out loud in that group, despite how comfortable I felt with everyone. I equated praying aloud to public speaking, and public speaking has always sent me into a panic attack. I'd rather do almost anything else. Praying aloud is almost more challenging for me, because not only am I speaking in front of a group, but also I'm being vulnerable when I talk to God. My time with this group of women helped me get rid of that fear and realize the only thing that matters is that I'm genuine with the Lord when speaking to Him.

Those women and I haven't seen each other in almost a year and a half now, yet we still communicate regularly as a group, sharing prayer requests and praises and motherhood advice. Military life has us scattered all around the globe now, but it's so wonderful to know we have a group of women we can turn to, who will never judge us and can offer biblical advice about how to tackle anything we're going through. If they don't have any wise words, they'll pray for us. And we know they're really praying, not just saying they will. We confide in each other and encourage each other, and there's never any fear of being judged or ridiculed. We're children of God, and we love and respect each other for that.

After my time with those amazing women in Guam, we moved to Virginia, and God came through again, giving me yet another great group of sisters in Christ to lean on. The biggest blessing of all was my neighbor, Sidney, who taught me so much about being a Christian wife and mother. Sidney isn't afraid to talk to anyone about Jesus. She'd tell a lamppost about Jesus, and I mean that in the best way. I am in awe of her bold faith. Sidney seems to look at every situation from a biblical perspective, and she really helped me start to live that way. Plus, she introduced me to the rest of the women who became a close-knit group. She was my "Lana" in a new location.

I can be shy and slow to make friends in a new situation, so it helps to find someone outgoing who can kind of force me into social situations I might otherwise avoid. Sidney did that for me in Virginia, inviting me to Women of the Chapel and MOPS the first day I met her. Women of the Chapel is a weekly Bible study found on most military bases. MOPs stands for Mothers of Pre-schoolers and is a Christian-based organization for moms of young kids who meet twice a month while someone else watches their kids. WOC and MOPs pulled me out of my shell, boosting both my social confidence and my spiritual confidence, and a lot of that had to do with that group of women who attended both and became my sisters. As in Guam, each woman brought something different to the table that we all could learn from. Most of us had kids, but some didn't. Some of us had gone through husbands deploying, but some hadn't. Some of us had been walking with the Lord most of our lives, but some were babies in their relationship with Christ. Some of us dealt with miscarriages and infertility. Some of us dealt with problems with our husbands. Some of us had problems with family members.

We all had things we could share advice about because we experienced it or *ask* advice about because we were starting to go through it. And again, all of it was wrapped in biblical wisdom and prayer. I felt as if the Holy Spirit was present whenever we had a serious conversation in that group of women. We prayed for each other and with each other, and still do to this day, even though we're scattered across the country now.

One of the cool things this group did was what I like to call the Circle of Truth. Whenever someone was about to move away, we'd get together one last time and do what became a tradition of going around the circle and speaking truth about the woman who was leaving. I think we as women have a hard time believing positive truths about ourselves, but when it comes from friends, especially godly friends, it makes it easier to believe. I don't remember which one of us started it, but I know God put it on her heart to do this round-robin complimenting session to help us understand who God made us to be. The goal was to go deeper than your average, surface-level compliments. We tried to dig deep and tell this woman something she needed to hear about herself. When it was my last day with the group and they took turns talking about me, I was shocked at what they had to say. Here are just a few of the things said about me:

"She has the gift of transparency. She helped me be open and talk about anything. She's super organized, and that inspires me. She relies on prayer so much." This surprised me because I feel I struggle sometimes with being genuine, and I have to stop myself from trying to fit in, even among Christian women. It was so encouraging for me to hear that she perceived me as being transparent. And she really knew me after living next door to me for a year, so it wasn't as if I'd pulled the wool over her eyes. I was also shocked to be called "super organized," because I usually feel like a big old mess. And I was surprised that she thought I relied on prayer "so much," because I often feel I don't pray nearly enough. She had unknowingly encouraged me in some of my insecurities.

Other words used to describe me were "sweet spirit," "gentle demeanor," "calm personality." I'm sorry, what? Me? I wanted to ask if they were sure they knew who they were describing. I rarely, if ever, would describe myself as calm or gentle. In fact, I feel like a raging lunatic 90 percent of the time in my own home. I wrestled with these descriptions for a while. How could multiple people think I possessed these traits? I seriously doubt my husband or children would describe me this way. I wondered if I was putting on some kind of act in front of my friends and being the real me at home. But after some prayer and soul-searching, I believe God showed me that these women knew the real me.

They'd spent a year with me, studying the Bible, praying together, sharing our most vulnerable stories. The "mommy monster" at home was not the real me. That's just a woman who's a product of postpartum hormones, lack of sleep, and annoying children. That's a woman who too easily lets the enemy get the best of her in stressful situations. But that's also a woman who can be better, who can be more than a victim of her hormones or stress level. Those sisters in Christ spoke so much truth and encouragement to me that day. It made me want to be that person they were describing all the time, not just in an easy situation, hanging out with my besties.

> *And let us consider how we may spur one another on toward love and good deeds, not giving up meeting together, as some are in the habit of doing, but encouraging one another—and all the more as you see the Day approaching* (Hebrews 10:24-25).

I encourage women in Bible study groups to start doing the Circle of Truth. Let's encourage one another! If you're in a group of women studying God's Word, or even just a group of friends, give it a try. Start with one person and go around the room, with each person speaking about her strengths. It's also a good idea to have someone write it all down, so she can refer to the kind and uplifting words. You'll be amazed at the fruit God brings from it.

The other cool thing that happened because of my relationship with a group of godly women was how my husband found a group of godly men he could relate to—my friends' husbands. The Lord had been working in Michael ever since he got sober about five years before we moved to Virginia. I had seen proof of Michael's spiritual growth, but it was at a different rate than mine. God convicted us about different things at different times, and

I trusted His timing. But sometimes it was frustrating to feel so inspired about making changes in our family or marriage that came from God, only to find out God wasn't prompting Michael in the same way. Then, in Virginia, it was as if Michael jumped in the fast lane.

Suddenly, he was surrounded by Christian men who were also tough Marines. They could talk about Jesus and still talk about sports and guns and other guy stuff. These were guys Michael could relate to in many ways, and they were also guys who could speak knowledgeably about the Bible and pray out loud in front of a large group. They'd talk about how "cool" the battles were in the Old Testament, and then they'd give testimonies about some sensitive subjects. I think that was a real turning point for Michael, seeing real men who were just like him, comfortably talking about Jesus and salvation.

That's why I think it's so important to surround yourself with fellow Christians. I have seen how much a person can grow when they spend their time with other believers. Our marriage grew as we watched how other Christian marriages worked and how those couples handled tough situations. We both found confidence in praying out loud in a group setting, which before our time in Virginia was uncomfortable for both of us. Our conversations changed, taking on a more biblical approach to every subject. The Lord opened our eyes during our time with that group of people, showing us that any preconceived notions we had about people walking with the Lord were probably wrong. They were people just like us, having kids, creating homes, fighting with each other, trying to stay on top of their finances, and all that. But they showed us how much better life is, how much joy you can find, when you take a biblical approach to everything. When you pray about everything. When you look to the Lord for guidance on everything.

Do not be deceived: "Bad company ruins good morals" (1 Corinthians 15:33).

Whoever walks with the wise becomes wise, but the companion of fools will suffer harm (Proverbs 13:20).

As iron sharpens iron, so a friend sharpens a friend (Proverbs 27:17).

I do want to take a moment and add that there's something to be said for having nonbelieving friends in your life or other believers who aren't walking with the Lord. If we don't engage with the world, we won't change the world. How can we bring the gospel to as many as possible if we don't ever interact with people who don't know the gospel?

For a long time, I was scared to talk about Jesus with nonbelievers because I felt I didn't know enough to have an intelligent conversation about Him. But God has spent the last couple of years changing my point of view on that. While He has increased my knowledge of the Bible and Christ's story, He's also taught me that I don't need to rely on my own intelligence or way with words if I'm talking to someone about Him. God will give me the words and the opportunity to say them. Or He won't, and I'll know that it wasn't the right time.

About six weeks after we moved to Florida, my brother-in-law came to visit us. He is not a believer, and his need for salvation has weighed heavily on me for years. About halfway through our time in Guam, God seemed to tell me that I needed to start praying for my brother-in-law's salvation. I didn't know why then, and I don't know why now. But I thought maybe I'd have some role to play in planting a seed that would lead him to Christ. It's an uphill road with him, though. It's not as if he's never heard the gospel. He grew up in a Christian family, and he rejected all of it. He speaks out against Christians, but that didn't scare me. As his Florida visit was approaching, I felt God was putting it on my heart to have a conversation with him about his salvation. I was nervous, but I prayed leading up to that visit and felt confident that this was what I was supposed to do.

Then he arrived. We hung out several times over a few days, and not once did I feel it was the time to start talking about Jesus. I never had a moment when it seemed right. It wasn't as if I got nervous and backed out. I just never felt as if I could bring it up naturally, and if it was forced, I knew he wasn't going to listen. I was disappointed, because I'd done all this spiritual preparation for it. But in the end, I know God didn't present the opportunity; therefore, that wasn't the timing God wanted. So, I continue to pray for my brother-in-law and wait for God to show me my role in his journey to Jesus.

If we never engage with the world, or if we never let our kids engage with the world, we won't be able to bring Jesus to the world. We won't be able to prepare our children for being *in* the world but not *of* the world. It's getting harder and harder for Christians to be in this fallen world, but our God is faithful and will always sustain and protect us. Let's be good soldiers and get out there and fight for Him.

Part of being a good Christian soldier means we guard our hearts and minds as well:

"More than anything you guard, protect your mind, for life flows from it" (Proverbs 4:23).

In this current age of social media, our "friends" are not just the people we see face to face. We have to be careful about our interactions on social media as well. It's important to be mindful of who you follow on Facebook, Twitter, or Instagram.

Let's go ahead and admit we spend way too much time on these sites. I like to justify it sometimes by thinking about how previous generations of women may have spent the same amount of time watching television or flipping through magazines. We've just changed what kind of media we consume. The point is, our brains are filled with whatever we see throughout our day.

Are you reading mostly political posts that breed constant negativity? Are you looking at pictures of Photoshopped women or seemingly perfect celebrities? Or are you following Christian writers and speakers and getting a continual dose of scripture and biblical encouragement? For me, my Twitter feed is my main source of content. My Facebook feed is mostly friends and family posting baby pictures and funny cat memes. But Twitter is where I've gone for news and entertainment for quite a few years now.

About a year ago, I realized that every time I finished reading my Twitter feed, I felt low. I had somehow filled my feed with politics and celebrity news, none of which was doing anything to teach me to be more like Christ or remind me of the hope found in Jesus. I swore off Twitter for a little while but then discovered how many inspirational Christians are on there! I unfollowed the majority of the accounts that filled my feed with negativity and replaced them with Beth Moore, Priscilla Shirer, The Christian Post, Faithwire, and others in that genre.

When I hop on Twitter during breakfast each morning, I'm greeted by uplifting scripture, biblical commentary, and great reminders about how believers should be living their lives. I know some people think we should give up social media altogether, but I think it can do a lot of good if it's used correctly. If your time on social media is bringing you down instead of lifting you up, go clean up that follow list and plug in some truth-tellers who can encourage you as a sister in Christ.

Chapter 8

Get Up!

I've talked about what an amazing time our year in Virginia was, with our wonderful group of friends and growth as a couple. But that was also a hard year for me personally. When we moved into our house in Virginia, we'd just finished several weeks of traveling and living out of suitcases, with three kids, a dog, and a cat. We returned to the States after three years in Guam and had a lot of catching up to do with family. Half our family had never met our two youngest children, since they were both born in Guam. So we spent a week with Michael's dad and stepmom, followed by a week with my mom, followed by a week with friends in Tallahas-

see, followed by a week with my dad in North Carolina. This all came after spending our final two weeks in
Guam in a hotel.

We'd been living out of suitcases without a home of
our own for about six weeks before finally making it to
our new home in Virginia. Our baby, Ava, was only three
months old when we left Guam, so she was still a very
small and needy baby during that summer of traveling, and
I was in the thick of postpartum hormones and emotions.

I try to look back on that summer fondly, as a time
the Lord was strengthening and refining me. But it is
hard to see any joy in those months. We moved to a new
spot every week. We had three kids and two pets to try
to make comfortable and entertain in houses that had no
toys or anything for entertaining kids. In fact, most of the
places we went to had a lot of things kids could easily
break. It was exhausting. (I may be exaggerating a bit to
say there was no joy. We did make some good memories
with family, and it was nice to see them again after living
halfway around the world for so long. But it was *so hard*
to not be in our own home for that long.)

By the time we got to Virginia, I was exhausted
and beyond stressed out. I'd had no breaks. No time
to myself. No time alone with Michael. Our cups were
empty, and there was no time to fill them back up. We had
to move into and set up our new home. It was August,

so school was starting, and we needed to find a school and ballet studio for Kelly. Plus, we lived right outside Washington, DC! There was so much to see and do, and we only had a year to do it all, so we filled our weekends with trips into the capital. I jumped right in to Women of the Chapel and MOPs, so my free days were quickly filling up too. And there's the whole business of running a household: cooking, cleaning, laundry, grocery shopping, and everything else. I was majorly running on empty, and it was starting to show.

I snapped at Michael. I snapped at the kids. I cried a lot. I felt an overwhelming amount of mom guilt over how often I yelled at the kids. I was hanging on by a thread, with a smile on my face. I was making friends, but I didn't feel close enough to any of them to confess my struggles as a mom and wife. I didn't even want to talk to Michael about it. I complained to him about day-to-day annoyances, but I never disclosed the extent to which I was suffering. I don't know if it was postpartum depression or just a lack of taking time for myself, but something was wrong, and I didn't know how to fix it.

Once again, I'm looking back at a tough situation in which I forgot to pray! I was praying regularly for my friends and family, and I probably asked God for help with my motherhood struggles from time to time. But I wasn't relying on God for strength. I wasn't expecting Him to be the one to save me and turn things around. Once again, I was trying to do it on my own, and I was failing.

Until one night in early December. It had been a particularly bad day with the kids, and I was drowning in my mom guilt. I felt I had yet again been the worst mom ever. I was convinced I was ruining my kids for life, and thanks to some Facebook article, I was also convinced that I'd already ruined the lives of my grandchildren. All my yelling and impatience was going to trickle down through the generations. I was solely responsible for ruining my family for decades to come! (Insert eye-roll emoji. Pity party much?)

That night I took a shower, and I just let it all go. I fell to my knees in that steamy tub and sobbed out loud to God, begging Him to help me change, help me break the cycle of yelling in my family, help me be the kind, gentle, merciful, patient mother He'd created me to be. I knew He wanted me to stay at home with my kids in this season, so I knew He would help me through it. After that tearful shower of repentance and submission, a peace came over me. I had no doubt God was going to help me get through this tough season.

But God can be unpredictable. I assumed He was going to send me some kind of help with the kids or maybe a regular opportunity to take some time for myself and get some pampering or something that would fill my cup. Instead, He called me closer to Him. Sometime around the end of December, He put it on my heart that it was time to give up the idol of sleep and start waking up with Him each morning.

The idea of getting up early to study the Bible and spend time in prayer had been recommended to me many times. But as someone who was either pregnant or nursing for the last six years, the idea of giving up even five minutes of precious sleep seemed ludicrous, even if it was to spend time with the Lord. I had barely slept in years! Why, oh why, would I *voluntarily* get up early for anything? I could do Bible study and prayer time during naptime every day or after the kids went to bed. Why did I need to start my day that way when it meant getting up so early?

But then. Ah, the "but then." A good friend who had no clue I was fighting this idea of getting up early with the Lord introduced me to the concept of sleep being an idol. An idol is anything we put above the Lord, right? Well, I was certainly putting sleep above time with the Lord in the morning. And now that God had prompted me to get up early and begin my day in His Word, I was not only letting sleep become an idol, but also I was straight up being disobedient. So, I made a decision. On January 1, 2018, I would start waking up at the ridiculous hour of 5:30 a.m. to spend time with God and study His Word.

It's hard to describe what a difference that made. I can't even pinpoint what changed. So many things just got a little easier. I spent thirty minutes at the start of each day reading the Bible, journaling about what I'd read, and then praying. I got a great journal that guided me through some readings and helped me learn how to pray for things beyond my own needs. And the coolest part was that I didn't feel exhausted throughout the day, as I assumed I would if I got up that early. The Lord sustained me because I was being obedient.

I started to learn the stories of the Bible. Key verses implanted themselves in my brain, and I was able to call on them in times of need. Feeding my mind and soul with His Word first thing in the morning changed my mindset for the entire day. I'm not trying to pretend that everything was perfect all of a sudden. But I felt something had shifted, and I was better prepared to handle each day's challenges. I noticed the difference the most on the days when it didn't happen. If I woke up late and didn't get in my early-morning time with God, the whole day felt off.

Then, around the first of March, I went on a Christian women's retreat. I cannot say enough good things about this experience. If you have a chance to go on a retreat, especially one where you travel away from home for a few nights, *do it*. It's so incredible to spend multiple days fully immersing yourself in the Word and worship music and Christian fellowship. I almost didn't go, because I didn't know any of the women all that well, and that was enough to let my social anxiety win and keep me home. But the Lord wasn't having that. The nudge on my heart was persistent, and I knew I had to go.

I got to know some amazing women who showed me that I wasn't alone in my struggles as a wife and mom. We sang worship songs, did devotionals, held group prayer circles, and had independent time with the Lord. We ate our meals together and shared hotel rooms. I heard from older women who'd already made it through the tough baby season. I heard from women in the thick of babies and toddlers but with a different approach. I heard from mothers of children with health struggles that put my own issues into perspective. I confided in a seasoned mom, who gave me wonderful, biblical advice on how to handle my struggle with yelling and impatience. And I participated in a karaoke dance party that left us all feeling as if we were sixteen again.

I came home from that retreat with my cup full and running over. I felt like a new woman! I was full of patience, grace, and kindness toward my kids, no matter what they threw at me, both figuratively and literally. And it lasted past that first day back home! I assumed I would feel better after the retreat and be able to apply what I'd learned for a day or two, maybe even a week. But I never imagined it would last for weeks, months even. Sure, I had rough days here and there like everyone else. But overall, I had a different outlook on motherhood after that retreat, which is a testimony to how God will bless us and sustain us when we focus on His principles for how to live our lives. We can't spend our long days as mothers of little ones focusing on the negative and reacting with anger and impatience.

But the fruit of the Spirit is love, joy, peace, forbearance, kindness, goodness, faithfulness, gentleness and self-control. Against such things there is no law (Galatians 5:22-23).

God wants us to live out the fruit of the Spirit in our homes, in our families, and with our husbands and children. When we let the opposite of that fruit get the best of us, things start to go downhill. So now, on the tough days, I try to remember what I learned from my sisters in Christ at that retreat, and I focus on those nine fruits of the Spirit, trying to live out at least one of them.

In fact, my morning prayers frequently include, "God, help me live out the fruits of the Spirit today," usually focusing on gentleness and self-control. I don't know about you, but as a mother of young kiddos, I find those two to be the hardest to keep front and center. There's just something about hearing "mommy" for the 870th time today or repeating "put your shoes on" fifty-five times before it's heard that makes it hard to remain gentle and in control.

So I pray for help with that in the morning. And as we get in the car to head to school. And as I'm starting to grumble around dinner time. And as I lay my head down at night.

Sometimes we just have a *day*. I remember one night after dinner in Florida during that horrid bed-and-bath time when my husband suggested I take a walk to cool my head, because I had turned into Super Mommy Monster, spitting venom at anyone in my path. I certainly don't always remember to live out the fruit of the Spirit. I don't want you to think I'm getting it right all the time. I'm human, and I still mess it up. My flesh still wins out, and I lose my cool, hurting everyone around me. But that's where grace comes into play. Where would we be without God's grace? Probably crying in the fetal position on the bathroom floor, wondering how we'd ever come back from that awful thing we just said to our husband/child/parent/friend/sibling in the heat of the moment. Praise God for grace!

Chapter 9

Run, Chrissie, Run

God continued to chisel away at my worldly exterior throughout our last few months in Virginia. His next goal? Turn me into a health-conscious runner. (Insert hysterically laughing emoji here.) Let me tell you a few things about my physical condition. First of all, I'm naturally thin (please don't hate me). But most of my adult life, I've been a pretty unhealthy thin person. I haven't dealt with any major illnesses or diseases, but I have not been a model for how to live a healthy life.

My problem is sweets. I adore them in any fashion. Chocolate, vanilla, savory, sour, hot, cold; you can't go wrong with almost any kind of dessert. Sweets led to some serious weight gain during all three of my pregnancies. Sweets have led to some not-so-fun moments at the dentist. And sweets were probably destroying the inside of my body without my knowledge. I never thought twice about how much sugar I consumed, because I never gained weight unless I was pregnant. And to top it off, I never exercised. I did ballet my entire childhood and into college, and it was a serious endeavor for me for a long time. My last two years of high school, my dance instructors wanted me to put on some muscle, so I started going to the gym every day for a while there. My going to the gym usually consisted of using the elliptical machine for about twenty minutes and then pretending I knew what I was doing on the weight equipment for a while, followed by a lot of stretching in front of a mirror. I would have benefited from a trainer, but that wasn't in the cards at the time.

Once I hit college and realized I was never going to be the type of ballerina I'd always dreamed of, I quit dancing. And I quit all forms of physical activity at the same time. For the next twelve years, I did some yoga here and there, and I think I tried running once sometime around 2008. I even went hiking a few times with Michael, but I despised exercise in general. It wasn't fun for me. Especially running! I'd probably pick any other form of exercise over running. And then.

In April of our year in Virginia, I took the kids to visit my dad and stepmom for a week while Michael stayed behind for work. My dad and stepmom are conscious of everything they put in their bodies and had recently given up all added sugars in their diet. I spent that week discussing this new way of eating and hearing how it was improving so many aspects of their lives. I was drawn to the idea, because I'd recently heard a cancer survivor speak about the effects of sugar on her body and how it had invited the cancer right on in. But I told my dad there was no way Michael would go for such a drastic diet change. He'd never had any inclination to change his diet, no matter what his needs were. He'd exercise 'til the cows came home before giving up any of his favorite foods. And then.

I came home from that trip late on a Sunday afternoon to find Michael standing in a very clean kitchen—partly because he'd had a massive ginger beer explosion in the kitchen that weekend, but that's a story for another day. It was also clean because he had overhauled our pantry and fridge. Before I'd said a word about my week of sugar-free eating, he told me he felt it was time we revamped our eating habits and give up all added sugar. I kid you not, those were his exact words.

I just spent a week talking with my dad and stepmom about this exact diet change, and then I come home to find

Michael ready to make the change without any prompting from me? God is good! How else can you explain that? God knew it was time for Michael and me to start treating our bodies like temples (1 Corinthians 3:16), and we were ready. We changed our diet and stuck with it for a long time, even during our move to Florida. That was a true testament to our commitment to this lifestyle change and how God was sustaining us through it. He used us to encourage one another and help us stay on track.

As for that long drive from Virginia to Florida, I did not want to think about eating healthy food. In my mind, the trip was stressful enough already. Couldn't we just get fast food along the way and then regain our healthy eating habits once we got there? But God had lit a fire under Michael, and he wasn't ready to give up this new way of eating, not even for a two-day road trip with three young kids.

We cooked chicken ahead of time and bought cheese and nuts and fruits and veggies and packed all of our meals in a cooler. We stayed on track and saved a fair amount of money. We've learned since then that moderation is a key to success, so we aren't as strict as we were in the beginning. But that allows us to practice giving ourselves grace when we cheat and eat some ice cream or a couple of pieces of Halloween candy. It's also easier to stick with when you don't deprive yourself all the time.

God wasn't ready to stop at the diet change, though. One weekend around that same time, Clayton's Saturday morning soccer game was cancelled, so we all went down to the soccer field to kick the ball around and expend some energy. After we'd been there a while, my friend Emily showed up with her family. She was in the middle of a weight-loss challenge and was running laps around the track while her boys played on the soccer field. She asked me to run just one lap with her, and Michael egged me on. I agreed to one lap, because as I mentioned, *I am not a runner*. I did the lap, and lo and behold, I didn't feel as if I was dying afterwards! I kind of enjoyed it. And that was all the confidence I needed to jump-start my running routine.

I realize that may sound pretty weird. You're thinking maybe I wasn't so much against running after all if my mind changed that quickly, after just one lap around a track. But I'm not exaggerating about my disdain for running prior to that Saturday morning. God changed my heart in an instant. He was doing a work in me to get me healthy, and He gave me this massive 180 on my opinion toward running during that one lap. How else can you explain such a quick change of heart?

The next week, I started with just one mile. And that first mile was a killer. Our neighborhood was hilly, and one mile seemed to be a long way for this girl who'd seldom run before. It hurt, but I still loved it. It was such a weird feeling for me to look forward to running every day. I was so vehemently against running for so many years that I can only point to God as the source of my change of heart. He used my friend Emily to boost my confidence that day. He used Michael to keep me motivated in the weeks that followed, encouraging me to run just a little farther each time.

"You ran 1.5 miles today? Run two miles tomorrow," he'd say. I'd almost be annoyed by it, thinking that extra half mile was too much for me. But then I'd get out there the next day and get it done. It felt so good. I felt so accomplished. I had a new confidence in myself and in my body.

I knew Michael had hoped for an athletic wife, and I felt bad for dropping the ball on that. Now I felt more confident as a wife, because I was getting in shape and doing something with my husband. I felt more confident as a woman, because I could do things like run up the stairs to check on the baby without getting winded. And I felt a new confidence in my relationship with God. I was incredulous that I had kept up the running and hadn't found a reason to quit. My only explanation: God. He put a fire in me to get healthy, and I never want to turn back.

We moved to Florida a few months after this lifestyle change, and God provided me with an opportunity to up my game even more. Michael's best friend from childhood lived in our new town with his wife and four kids. They'd lived there for years, and his wife, Kristen, ran a fitness class out of her garage. Her class schedule lined up perfectly with Clayton's preschool schedule, and I was able to bring baby Ava along with me because Kristen's little ones hung out during class too. It couldn't have fit my life any better.

So, in addition to running three days a week and making better eating choices, now I could add a fitness class that worked on building muscle and stamina. And the class brought me to a new group of women, which was encouraging to find in a new place. We all had different ability levels, but we inspired each other to keep trying, keep building strength, keep working harder. I felt so well-rounded in this new world of taking care of my body only four months after I decided to make this change. I still can't believe how fast God worked in that area of my life. Isn't it amazing how powerful He is? When He wants something done in us, He makes it happen.

Looking back, I can see all the puzzle pieces He fit together to bring me to this place of wanting a healthy lifestyle more than I wanted chocolate cake, more than I wanted to lie around and watch Netflix instead of working out. Just like the way He led me to wanting early morning prayer time with Him more than I wanted to sleep. God will change us; we just have to be open and sensitive to His calling. As of this writing, the farthest I've run is a half marathon. Could a full marathon be in my future? That sounds a little impossible right now, until I remind myself that the God of the universe has my back, giving me the strength to get through each mile.

That strength comes in handy when I'm pushing myself to the limit. On more than one occasion, either during a rough run or an especially tiring workout class, I'll start repeating "In Your strength, not mine!" over and over in my head to get me to the end. Try it! It works.

Don't you know that you yourselves are God's temple and that God's Spirit dwells in your midst? If anyone destroys God's temple, God will destroy that person; for God's temple is sacred, and you together are that temple (1 Corinthians 3:16-17).

Therefore, I urge you, brothers and sisters, in view of God's mercy, to offer your bodies as a living sacrifice, holy and pleasing to God—this is your true and proper worship (Romans 12:1).

We're talking about giving ourselves grace here, right? Grace has proven to be a big factor when it comes to my new, healthy lifestyle. I was motivated and excited and committed to this thing in the beginning. And my motivation for exercise hasn't changed, which is funny because I thought that'd be the first place where I would slack off. But I've reached a point where I physically feel kind of blah if I skip my workout or my run. The eating, though. That's where I struggle, and I think it has to do with seeing results.

If I skip a workout or a run, I can feel a difference in my stamina and strength. If I eat candy every day for a week, I don't feel any real difference. Now, if I reverted my entire way of eating back to the carb- and sugar-filled diet it used to be, I'd definitely feel more tired and less energetic, and I'd probably get sick more often. But I can eat candy every day for a week and still feel fine.

I shouldn't be doing that, though. I made this commitment to a healthier life. I know all the bad side effects of filling your body with sugar. Yet, the sweets still call to me! It's an addiction, and I never understood how powerful it was until I had to give it up. Well, *chose* to give it up. But I feel I'm cheating on myself, cheating on Michael, and cheating on God when I eat all those sweets. I promised myself, Michael, and God that I would make this change. But again, I have to give myself grace.

A once-in-a-while cheat is fine, in my opinion, and makes it easier to stick to a healthier way of eating. But candy every day for a week is not the same thing as a small cheat. I choose to give myself grace on that because I don't think letting myself become consumed by guilt over all that candy is going to help me either. Grace keeps me going and lets me start over the next day, relying on God's strength to help me walk past that bucket of Halloween candy without touching those delicious Reese's Peanut Butter Cups. Why does everything that tastes good have to be full of sugar?

Have you noticed a common theme here? We're replacing guilt with grace. Every time. I don't see grace as an excuse to make a bad choice and then shrug it off. But it provides an opportunity to forgive yourself as God forgives you. And when you become more skilled at forgiving yourself, it'll be easier to forgive others too.

Chapter 10

All in Good Time

I t can be so easy to write off answered prayers as simple coincidences. And I get that if you don't have a higher power you believe is working for the good in your life, you have no way to explain why good things happen other than that they just happen. But once I accepted Jesus into my life and started learning about the Lord and the history of how He's working in the world, I felt there was no other way to explain it. It seems so obvious to me that I have God to thank, not only for all the good things that have happened to me but also for the timing of all the good things.

One of my favorite things to do is to look back at my life over the previous year and try to see where God was working and why He was doing it *at that time*. I believe He led me to boarding school when I was thirteen to get me away from a tough family life at home. At the time I thought He was leading me to a career as a professional ballerina, but that sure didn't pan out. I think He was teaching me independence and maturity at a young age, so I didn't need to rely on my family much longer.

I don't mean to sound ungrateful for what my family did for me at that time, but I think God wanted me to distance myself from them early on so I would be prepared to be distanced from them later. I was never destined to be the girl who lived two streets over from her parents her whole life. I love my parents, and I'd love to see them more often than I currently do. But God knew that wasn't in the cards in His plans for me to become a military wife, so He started preparing me early on.

I believe God led me to give up the ballet dream my freshman year in college so I could meet my husband. If I had remained a dance major, I never would have had time for a waitressing job at Ruby Tuesday, where I met Michael. Sure, God could have introduced us in a million other ways, but having us work together for years formed this bond that couldn't be broken, even when the relationship itself was in troubled waters. We may get into a fight on Wednesday evening, but then we'd still have to put a smile on our faces at work together on Thursday, and I think that got us through some hard times during those early years.

I believe God brought me to a job at the local television station in Tallahassee right after college so I could stay in town until Michael graduated and still be furthering my career. In fact, I think God gave me quick promotions within that job so I wouldn't start looking for a job in another city or bigger market. He knew I needed to stay with Michael, and Michael couldn't leave Tallahassee until he graduated two and a half years after I did.

One of the times God moved in a major way in my life was when He gave Michael his first duty station in Alamogordo, New Mexico. Never heard of it? Neither had I. Let's go back to that summer evening in Biloxi, Mississippi, when we learned we were about to head west. Michael had been living in Biloxi for about six months, going to tech school at Keesler Air Force Base. I stayed in Tallahassee to keep my job because he would only be gone for six months.

His school had what's called a drop night, when all the students' assignments "drop" and they find out where they're about to spend the next three years. They try to make it fun, so the theme was Wheel of Fortune. Each student would go up and find a certain number of blank spots for letters on the board. They'd guess letters until they could figure out the name of the base where they would be stationed.

When it was Michael's turn, he went up and immediately guessed "H." Michael and I both had big dreams of moving to Hurlburt Air Force Base in the Florida panhandle. It was only a couple of hours away from all our friends and family in Tallahassee. Our parents lived in Florida, so it'd be easy to see them frequently. Plus, Michael's best friend was already stationed at Hurlburt, so basically, it would be a dream come true. You can imagine our excitement when that "H" did fill up the first blank space on the board. We jumped for joy! It was happening! This Air Force thing wasn't so bad after all. What an easy transition it was going to be!

And then. Michael guessed "U" and…nothing. Our excitement-filled balloon quickly deflated. It wasn't Hurlburt, and we couldn't even think of another base that started with "H." Michael just started guessing random letters until he got Holloman. I had to Google it to find out it was located in Alamogordo, New Mexico. New Mexico? Was that even a real state? I'd never even known anyone who *visited* New Mexico, much less lived there. I'd never been west of the Mississippi! It was a shock, to say the least. I put a smile on my face and tried to look at it as an adventure like most military wives do when they find out they're moving to the middle of nowhere for three years, but I was bummed. I was so sure we were going to Florida that I hadn't entertained the idea of going somewhere else. Ah, how naïve of me. It makes me chuckle to think back on being a new military spouse.

God knew what He was doing. He isolated us in New Mexico, and that forced us to look at our problems head-on and deal with them. God took us out of our element, away from our friends and the way of life we'd known for years. It left me with a lot of time to soul search and see what kind of person I was. I didn't love what I discovered about myself, and I think that got me started on the long road to my salvation. I also don't believe Michael would have found sobriety if we had moved to Hurlburt, and he'd been surrounded by the same people he'd always hung out with. His heavy drinking would have still looked like social drinking, and the problem would never have been addressed. Once we were isolated and he was drinking alone, he was able to see the demon for what it was. Moving to New Mexico seemed like such a bummer when it happened, but looking back now, I know it was one of the biggest blessings in our lives. It also happens to be the birthplace of my firstborn, so it will always hold a special place in my heart.

When I think about it, I can see every duty station as a blessing from the Lord. I was excited about moving to Guam from the moment I knew it was happening. I wasn't scared of being so far from friends and family until I was in the thick of it, but God used that fear to mold and chisel me into a better wife and mother who has a true relationship with Him. That's not to say I couldn't have accomplished those things if I'd stayed right here in the States. But I believe God pushed me as far away as Guam, halfway around the world from my friends and family, so I had no one to rely on but Him, especially when He sent Michael away from me on a deployment.

I had some of my lowest moments during the time I was alone in Guam with Kelly and Clayton. I don't remember all of it; I think I blocked out some of it. But God reached down and pulled me out of that hole, and I came into the light wanting nothing more than to be close to Him. I craved it the way I crave a giant piece of molten lava chocolate cake. That craving came out of desperation for fundamental change in the kind of person I was. I had no doubt that the path to change came solely from the Lord. I learned all of that because of how alone I was in Guam.

Then came Virginia and a lesson on the value of community. Michael and I always said we'd never live on base, because we wanted a separation between job and family life. But God led us to live on base in Virginia, and because of that, we made the sweetest friends who helped us grow so much as Christians. Our kids were surrounded by other Christian kids in our neighborhood and experienced discipline from other Christian parents. It was a time of growth for our entire family.

And seven years after that Wheel of Fortune drop night in Biloxi—wouldn't you know it?—we finally made it to Hurlburt. God answered our prayer for this duty station, but He did it in His time. This has been one of the biggest lessons on God's perfect timing. He didn't say "no." He just said "not yet." We weren't ready in 2011. When we moved there in 2017, with familiar surroundings that we would have had if we'd come seven years ago, we had become different people. We had the armor of God to hold us up and sustain us in situations that were full of temptations. We had a strong marriage built on biblical respect, so neither of us wanted to let the other one down in any way. We were happy and healthy, and Hurlburt seemed much more like a blessing; it may have been a curse seven years earlier.

Wait for the Lord; be strong, and let your heart take courage; wait for the Lord! (Psalm 27:14).

I've mentioned that I want to adopt a child into our family one day, and I haven't always been OK with God's timing on that. But when I look back at how perfectly His timing has played out in all the other aspects of my life, it gives me renewed confidence to wait for His timing on adoption. Every time I try to do something in my own time, it doesn't play out very well. But God's perfect timing leads us down the road to happiness.

Chapter 11

Welcome to the Neighborhood

I n our final weeks of the year we lived in Virginia, my girlfriends and I were getting together weekly to fellowship, study the Bible, and pray for one another. Almost all of us were moving away that summer, so we often talked about how we would gain our footing in a new location. We talked about the struggles that are common to military spouses and especially how difficult moving week can be.

Someone suggested bringing meals to new families in our neighborhoods the day they move into their house. That would take such a burden off the mom. She wouldn't have to cook dinner or order pizza, and it would provide an opportunity to meet the new neighbors and show them a friendly face. It's an opportunity to live out Jesus' love. So, we all agreed to do that after we'd settled into our new homes and watched other families arrive.

Michael and I decided to live off base when we got to Florida, so I wasn't automatically surrounded by other military families who were moving during the busy summer season. I was eager to serve up a meal to a family in need but didn't know of anyone moving into the neighborhood. About a month after we moved in, new neighbors arrived at the house next door! They were a military family! It was as if God had served them right up for me to participate in this meal ministry. But after a few days of that family being in their new house, I started to chicken out.

I have a bit of social anxiety, and the enemy was latching on to that. He put butterflies in my stomach. He put doubts in my head. What if they weren't friendly? What if they thought it was super weird for me to bring them dinner when I didn't even know them? What if they have dietary restrictions or allergies? Did it matter if I decided not to take dinner to them? They'd never be the wiser. I put it off. I didn't want to completely back out, so I just kept telling myself I'd do it the following week.

About a week later, I was out for a run, listening to my favorite Christian podcast, "She Speaks Stories." If you haven't listened to it, stop reading this and go listen now! It's that good. I've never been so inspired in so many ways, and it helps my running go by very quickly because I'm so enthralled with what I'm listening to.

The episode I listened to that day was about Jesus' command to love your neighbor as yourself and what that means in practical, day-to-day life. The woman telling her story posed the question, "What if 'love thy neighbor' meant your literal neighbors? The people who live in the houses all around you?" During most of the podcast they talked about how you can engage with your neighbors and bring Jesus into your neighborhood. I couldn't believe I was listening to this podcast at the same time I was backing out of serving my neighbors. It seemed clear that God was speaking to me. He didn't want me to chicken out. He wanted me to fight Satan and all his negativity. He wanted me to show Jesus' love to the people next door.

That happened on a Saturday evening. I decided I would take dinner to them Monday night. Then Monday rolled around, and it was a crazy day. I don't remember what exactly was going on, but for some reason, by the end of the day I knew taking dinner to my neighbors wasn't in the cards. It was one of those #momlife days. But I'd already bought everything needed to cook for them, so I resolved to do it the next day.

Wouldn't you know it? I woke up the next day and saw the moving truck in their driveway! It was the day all their household goods arrived! I couldn't have picked a better day to be cooking dinner for them! They were going to be exhausted and hungry by dinnertime. It was perfect. All the guilt I felt for putting off this meal ministry melted away. God's timing is perfect! He knew what day that moving truck was coming, and He prepared me for that day. He brought me that specific broadcast about loving your neighbor on the right day. Then He let my Monday get disrupted so I wouldn't take the meal a day early. Isn't He faithful and perfect?

I made a cheesy baked spaghetti, salad, and cookies and took it over to them late that afternoon, three kiddos in tow. The family was surprised and grateful. That meal helped start a friendship that led to their teenage daughter babysitting our kids. I'm so glad I listened to God and not the enemy. I'm so glad God paved the way for me to take dinner to them on the right night.

I think this lesson from the Lord speaks to two important things: We need to love our neighbors, and we need to be in tune with the Holy Spirit so we can follow God's path. It occurred to me recently that loving your neighbor as yourself should go far beyond being nice to other people. I always perceived that command as something that simple. Just be kind to everyone, and you're good. But I think if we want to show people what Christ's love looks like, and in turn, bring them to know Christ, we have to go beyond holding open doors or smiling at someone as we pass each other in the grocery store aisle. It needs to be more active than that. It's about going above and beyond for other people whenever we can.

Your literal neighbors are a great place to start. Wouldn't it make a difference in this world if every neighborhood was a tight-knit community? What if everyone got together on a regular basis, sharing food and laughs, and getting to know one another? I've only lived in one neighborhood where I experienced something close to that, and it made all the difference in our lives! My kids thrived being surrounded by people they knew well and felt comfortable with. My husband and I had other adults to talk to at the end of the day or on weekends. We felt so well-rounded. It can be hard to plan outings with other adults when we all have such busy schedules. But when our friends live right next door, it's much easier to hang out regularly.

I'm not suggesting you go throw a block party next weekend and expect your whole neighborhood to show up, ready to become best friends—though that could certainly happen! God can do anything, and instant neighborhood friends are not outside the realm of possibility.

Maybe you have enough boldness to invite everyone on your street to your house for a cookout next weekend. That would be amazing.

But you can also do something simpler and still show just as much love. Like taking dinner to a new neighbor or a neighbor who's been under the weather. Offer to mow the lawn of the elderly lady who can't do it herself. If you have kids and see another family on your street with kids, invite them over for a playdate. Just keep it simple and love your neighbor.

The other part of this is staying in tune with the Holy Spirit so you can hear God guiding you on *how* to love your neighbor. God speaks to us through the Holy Spirit.

The Helper, the Holy Spirit, whom the Father will send in my name, will teach you everything and make you remember all that I have told you (John 14:26).

It took a lot of prayer and studying God's Word before I started to recognize when the Holy Spirit was speaking to me. It's almost like training yourself to understand what seems to be your own thoughts and feelings. If a particular thought or feeling comes up repeatedly, I start to pay attention to it and figure out what it is. Then I'll ask God for confirmation that it's from Him, which could come in many forms, like a Bible verse or wise counsel from a friend or family member.

When I needed to start loving my literal neighbors, God first brought me the idea through conversations with my group of girlfriends. Then He brought me the podcast and finally the moving truck in the driveway on the exact day I wanted to bring them dinner. All those things worked together to confirm that God was speaking about how I should interact with my neighbors.

In John 14, the Holy Spirit is called the Helper. Let Him help you. Listen to Him and look for confirmation from the Lord on how He's guiding you. Then follow through! Don't let the enemy slip in and prey on your insecurities and doubts. I almost missed an opportunity to love my neighbor and follow that great command because I was listening to Satan's whispers of doubt. Remember that God's love is stronger than anything the enemy tries to bring against you.

Love the Lord your God with all your heart and with all your soul and with all your mind and with all your strength. The second is this: "Love your neighbor as yourself." There is no commandment greater than these (Mark 12:30-31).

Chapter 12

No Pressure, Mama

My children, Kelly, Clayton, and Ava, became my main focus as soon as each one was born. Some might argue that this is because I'm a stay-at-home mom, so my entire day almost always revolves entirely around them. But it feels like more than that. God gives us an incredible responsibility when He gives us children.

Children are a heritage from the Lord, offspring a reward from him. Like arrows in the hands of a warrior are children born in one's youth. Blessed is the man whose quiver is full of them (Psalm 127:3-5).

Our children are the people we have the most influence over, out of everyone we will ever meet. In most cases, they're with us practically every day for the first eighteen years of their lives. Once my first child, Kelly, became old enough to understand what I was saying and start imitating me, I was shocked at the level of influence I had over another human being. If she saw me cooking dinner, she would go to her toy kitchen and pretend to cook dinner. If she saw me doing sit-ups and push-ups in an attempt to get back in shape, she'd start doing her adorable baby version of sit-ups and push-ups. If I accidentally let a not-so-nice word slip when I stubbed my toe, you'd better believe she'd start saying that not-so-nice word often, especially in front of Grandma. (Why do they always repeat the worst stuff when Grandma's around?)

Each time we added a child to the family, a sense of overwhelming responsibility grew and probably rightfully so. Parents should feel the weight of their role in their kids' lives. When it was just Kelly at home, my anxiety over that responsibility usually concerned things like repeating bad words or being on my phone too much. When we added Clayton to the mix, and my postpartum hormones had me acting like a crazy person, my anxiety was focused on how my erratic behavior was probably going to shape them into psychopaths, or at the very least, I was dooming them to a life of yelling at their own kids one day. Then came my sweet and sassy Ava Grace.

"What if I name her Grace?" I thought, when we were trying to choose a name for our third child. Maybe if I literally put the word "grace" in her name, I'd finally remember to give the child grace when she messes up. Maybe if I'm screaming "Ava Grace Kenaston!" across the room when she's hitting her brother over the head with a toy hammer, I'll hear the word "grace" and remember how much grace she deserves. Or I'll remember how much grace God gives me each day as I fail at motherhood, and I won't be consumed by mommy guilt.

I think grace is what's missing in today's mommy culture. It seems as if many of us moms fall into two categories. The first mom puts on a big, fake smile and pretends as if she's doing just fine all the time. Her life looks perfect on social media, and she never confides in anyone about her struggles. She likes the appearance of having it all together, and she doesn't want anything to mess up that façade.

Then there is the mom who has gotten so good at talking about her flaws that her life has become one big complaint. All she does is talk about how she messes everything up all the time. She's very good at playing the victim. Her children are too whiny, too messy, too disobedient. Her husband is too busy, too unhelpful, too unsympathetic. It's as if she doesn't feel like trying anymore because she seems to always mess it up.

If you don't feel as if you fit into either of those categories, maybe you're the mom in the middle. The mom who sometimes seems perfect and sometimes seems like a hot mess. I think I might fall into that category. I'm either faking perfection on Facebook, or I'm whining about how hard #momlife is on Twitter. There's rarely that in-between, which is what most of real life consists of.

You know what is missing from all three of these mamas? Grace. The perfect mom needs to give herself grace when things don't look so perfect. God doesn't expect perfection from us. In fact, He says,

"As it is written: 'There is no one righteous, not even one." (Romans 3:10).

We're human, and we're going to mess things up from time to time. That's why we have to be grateful for God's grace that forgives us and lets us try again the next day. Or the next hour. Or the next minute.

The complaining mom needs to give herself some grace so she can step out of the shadow of her perceived flaws. Her flaws do not define her. Her successes do not define her. Only her salvation in Jesus Christ defines her—as a child of God. And children of God are guaranteed this astounding thing called grace! Let God's grace wash over you, shed a couple of tears if you need to, pray for Him to sustain you with His strength, and get up and try to do better.

The third type of mama, the in-between mama, needs grace too. Grace when she's putting on an act and trying to look perfect to the outside world. Grace when she feels like whining all day and running off to a sunny beach in Mexico.

For me, it **all** comes down to grace and not just in motherhood. As a wife, a daughter, a sister, a friend. It's hard to admit failure, and I've spent a ridiculous amount of time doing everything I could to prevent failure. I'm not sure how I became so obsessed with avoiding it. I can't pinpoint when it started to become such a big deal for me.

I've always been a planner who liked to be prepared for any scenario. But I think after I had kids, I felt as if I was letting down more than just myself if something came up and I wasn't prepared for it. It probably started with packing a diaper bag. We must have everything this baby could need! Diapers, wipes, toys, snacks, pacifiers, change of clothes, blankets, hats, and more. Never mind that we were only going to Walmart, where I could easily buy any of those things if we needed it and didn't have it.

Once we added numbers two and three, I had to be prepared for every situation that might arise with three kids at different stages. This meant diapers for one, training pants and pull-ups for another. Different kinds of toys based on different ages. Different kinds of snacks based on different ages. I basically needed to carry a suitcase so I could be prepared at all times.

That somehow carried over into preparing for my own life. I started obsessively checking my weather app so I would always be dressed correctly for any temperature or condition. (I might still do that.) I asked eight thousand questions about every outing so I would know what to bring for every possible situation. It was no fun to surprise me because I'd just complain about not being prepared. That crazy need to be so prepared for everything stemmed from a need to never fail at anything. I probably could use a few years of therapy to dig into why I'm so afraid of failure, but I'm trying to let go of that as much as I can.

As I've grown closer to the Lord, I've learned He will sustain us in such extraordinary ways, through some crazy situations. He might even intentionally put us through failures so we will learn something. They aren't necessarily failures in His eyes. He's a good, good Father, and He loves us so much that He wants us to grow into the amazing humans He's created us to be.

Sometimes that takes hard lessons, like forgetting the pacifier on a Walmart trip during a particularly difficult phase Ava went through, when she'd scream bloody murder through the entire shopping trip while simultaneously trying to launch herself out of the cart and into my arms. I thought of that as a massive failure on my part. I should have remembered the pacifier. I should have just done a grocery pickup order so we wouldn't have to go inside. (Can we just take a moment and praise the Lord for grocery pickup?) I should have done something differently to be better equipped to handle this nightmare.

What I finally realized was that I didn't need any earthly item to handle this situation. I needed the Lord. I needed His armor to fight the enemy, who was using everything he had to try to get me to react in an angry, impatient, unloving way. I needed His strength and wisdom to guide me on how to calm Ava down and get her to cooperate. Or maybe I needed His wisdom to nudge me into leaving the store and coming back later, something unthinkable for this planner who has a specific time set aside for grocery shopping and couldn't imagine not getting it done at that exact time. Regardless, I was interpreting this situation as a failure, instead of giving myself grace for just being in a hard moment or giving Ava grace for being eighteen months old and acting her age.

So maybe calling her Grace doesn't always help me to remember grace in the hard moments. But I'm always thankful that God never forgets to give me grace. Other than eternal salvation, I think grace is our biggest gift from God. He knows we're going to continually mess up. But if we turn to Him in those moments, we'll find grace and forgiveness and a new start.

Chapter 13

A Time to Fail

I've been trying to figure out which is more difficult: giving yourself grace or giving your kids grace.
Maybe they're equally challenging. Maybe the key is
to realize our kids can't do anything on their own any
more than we can. We all need God's strength and mercy.
This leads me to believe that imparting this wisdom to
our children is one of the most important things we
should do as Christian parents.

We live in a society in which failure seems to be
unacceptable. Actually, it's gone from unacceptable to
straight-up horrifying. It seems as if so many people struggle to cope if they fail at something or don't get what they

want. I may be oversimplifying things here, but it seems as if every child in a previous generation got a trophy just for showing up, and now that generation is grown and has a hard time when they lose. I assume this generation was reared by well-meaning parents who didn't enjoy their own parents' tough love, so they thought the best thing they could do for their kids was to shelter them from any pain or heartache. Your soccer team wasn't good enough to win the championship? That's OK; you still get a bright, shiny trophy, just for participating!

This sort of thing is happening at my child's elementary school too. She was one of the top three kids in her class to earn the most points for good behavior one month. She was supposed to get a special lunch with the teacher, which she was excited about. She came home from school that day and told me she didn't get a special lunch with the teacher because all the other kids were upset that they didn't get the special lunch too. Instead, everyone got to eat with the teacher, and Kelly didn't get any reward for her good behavior. What kind of lesson is that teaching these kids? If you don't work hard enough to win, don't worry, you'll still get the same prize as the winners. Where is the incentive to try hard for anything if everyone is always a winner?

I understand that we are saved by faith, not through works, but I'm not talking about a salvation issue here.

I'm talking about young children learning how to work hard for what they want instead of having things handed to them. In Proverbs 13:4 it says,

"The soul of the sluggard craves and gets nothing, while the soul of the diligent is richly supplied."

And that's just one of many Bible verses about working hard for what you need. Nothing is just handed to you if you don't put in any work.

If kids never learn how to deal with disappointment, they might do something crazy when they fail or are rejected by someone. And I think a lot of that could be avoided if they knew their identity in Christ and knew the extent of God's grace when they miss the mark.

Let's bring it back to my little ones. It's easy to get up on my high horse and wag my finger at the mamas who always shelter their little guys and girls from every failure. In reality, when one of my kiddos is about to mess up, every fiber of my being wants to rescue them from that failure and prevent the ensuing heartache. But if I did that, how would they ever learn to cope with that failure? Obviously, if they're about to fall off the top of the playground equipment that's six feet high, I'll rescue them. I'm not going to let them break a leg to learn a lesson.

But if my three-year-old is building a block tower, and he makes the bottom much smaller than the top, I'm not going to walk over there and correct him. He'll watch the tower fall, most likely get pretty mad about it, and then we have the opportunity to discuss trying again, with a new plan. It may seem like an overly simple example, but I think that's how the little ones learn. We tell them it's OK that the tower fell, it's not the end of the world, and assure them that they have another chance to build it again. As they get older, this can translate into bigger lessons, with siblings or friends. If Clayton hits Ava, he gets punished, but the punishment ends with a discussion about grace and a chance to try again. We make sure he understands how fortunate we are that God gives us grace for our mistakes and lets us give it another shot. Then we send him off to try being nicer to his sister.

I hope that as my kids grow, it will be ingrained in them that failure is not the end of the world, that grace is extended to us from our heavenly Father, and that we should not only be very grateful for it but also use that as an opportunity to try harder to be the kind of person God wants us to be.

All that being said, it is *not easy* to give our children grace all the time. It depends on the severity of what they did, what kind of mood they're in, what kind of mood

I'm in, who's hungry or tired—all kinds of things play into whether I'm capable of giving them grace for their mistakes. And I admit that sometimes I forget about grace entirely, and I'm just angry. After the eight-hundredth time saying "clean up the playroom," I start to grow weary and forget all about giving them grace for being little kids who just want to play. Occasionally, yelling "Ava Grace!" will help, as I hoped it would. But more often than not, I remember the grace part later, when I'm feeling guilty for yelling at my kids, and I'm full of mommy guilt.

In that moment, God gently reminds me not only to give my children some grace but also to give myself grace. If they're allowed to mess up, so am I. It all hinges on how we act afterward. Who needs to apologize? Who needs to humble themselves and admit they messed up? Sometimes it's the kids. Sometimes it's me. Sometimes it's everyone. I'm sure some mothers will argue that apologizing to your kids shows weakness and teaches them that they have some control over you. But I think it teaches a reliance on the Lord. If I say I'm sorry, admit a mistake, and tell them I need God to help me too, I'm hoping that lesson will stay with them as they grow. I don't ever want them to think they're too old to need the Lord's help. Sometimes I feel as if the older I get, the *more* I need His help.

Another component of this is making sure my kids know who they are as children of God and what that means about their identity. I predict this will get harder as they get older, but we're just now entering the "mean girl" territory with my oldest, Kelly. She's come home from school a handful of times saying some of the girls were mean to her or didn't want to play with her. My initial mama bear reaction is to find these girls and give them a real stern talking-to! But that is not realistic and would probably only make matters worse. (I just want to protect my sweet baby girl!)

I hope that if she knows how much God loves her and how important that is, the sting of the girls' mean words won't be as painful. She's five years old, and I don't think she can quite grasp this concept. She knows who God is and how much He loves us, but it's not a love she can hear, see, or touch, so I'm not sure it means much to her yet. I pray daily that if I say it enough, she will start to believe it. I want it ingrained in her heart that her worth is as a child of God, not as Erica's best friend.

I did not grow up with this confidence as a child of God. I was a Christian, but I did not understand the extent of God's love. Mean words from classmates hurt me quite a bit. I can remember a lot of those hurtful words to this day. I'd give anything to go back to that difficult time and feel as loved by God as I do now. As parents, we have a chance to give our children that feeling of being loved. We can live as examples of His love by giving them grace during failures and boosting their confidence during heartache. We can be honest about our own mistakes and show them how God has given us another chance, thanks to His never-ending love and grace.

Let us have confidence, then, and approach God's throne, where there is grace. There we will receive mercy and find grace to help us just when we need it (Hebrews 4:16).

But the grace that God gives is even stronger. As the scripture says, "God resists the proud, but gives grace to the humble" (James 4:6).

Breathe in His grace, breathe out His praise.

Chapter 14

"It Doesn't Matter, It's in the Past"

God's unending grace applies to our past as well, our "before Christ" or "BC" life, as some people call it. Many adult believers have a past—a time when we weren't walking with the Lord and made some bad decisions. For me, that time was high school and college. I was away from home at boarding school without any spiritual guidance, and I did as much as I could get away with.

In high school, I smoked, cut class, sneaked out of my dorm, and found too much of my worth in boys and their opinions of me. My personality was based on whichever friend I was closest to at the time. I was also attending an art school, so it was easy to say that the drugs helped make our art better, whatever that means. I wasn't doing anything too crazy, but for a while there, marijuana was part of my daily life. I also gave up my purity before I left high school, to a guy I never saw again after graduation.

In college, I gave up the drugs but discovered alcohol. I partied my little heart out and still put way too much effort into attracting and impressing guys. I was an awkward adolescent who definitely didn't turn any boys' heads until I reached college. I was so tired of rejection at that point that I found my worth in any boy who found me attractive.

The crazy thing is, I was able to do all these things and still keep up with all my responsibilities, in both high school and college. All that stuff was fun and felt good, and I rarely suffered any consequences. I got caught smoking cigarettes once in high school. The school called my parents, and I got yelled at over the phone, but I was away at boarding school, and there wasn't a lot they could do.

In college, I kept my grades up and graduated magna cum laude, despite how much and how often I was drinking. I even had a job in my career field before I graduated. When there are few consequences for your bad behavior and you don't know the Lord, it's easy to keep behaving badly. Years later I realized how much I must have been breaking God's heart during that time. It breaks my own heart to think about my daughters acting that way.

If we confess our sins, he is faithful and will for-give us our sins and purify us from all unrighteousness (1 John 1:9).

But here's the good news. When you accept Jesus as your Savior and ask God for forgiveness, it's as if all that bad behavior is erased, or better yet, it can be used as part of your testimony to help others understand the beauty of God's love and acceptance. Jesus died on the cross and shed His blood *for you* so all your sins would be forgiven. Every single one of them. You get a clean slate and a new chance to live for the Lord. It truly is amazing grace. The lyrics "I once was lost but now I'm found, was blind but now I see" perfectly describe what redemption is like.

During my high school and college years, I was lost and blind. I had no concept of all the Lord had done for me and knew nothing about living for Him instead of for myself. And truth be told, I was not happy during that time. Sure, I had a lot of fun experiences and plenty of happy moments, but when I compare that time to how I feel now as a daughter of the King, it doesn't com-pare. It's as if there's a common thread of unhappiness through all those early years, but I can also look back and see how God never left my side. He was always guiding me and nudging me back into His arms.

All the grace He bestowed on me makes it easy for me to want to live for Him now. But I understand that this is a foreign concept for someone who isn't saved. Why would you live your life for an intangible God? But once you develop a true relationship with the Lord, you can't deny all the things He's done for you. All His blessings become apparent, and you're overwhelmed with gratitude. It's the very least I can do to live for Him.

I've seen how badly things can go when I start living for myself and following my own plans. In turn, I've seen how well things go when I follow God's guidance and do His bidding. It doesn't feel like an obligation. In my heart of hearts, I *want* to do what He asks. I want His guidance in my life. I love Him so much. He doesn't feel intangible to me.

Imagine you had a friend who sacrificed his only son so you could live forever. Just take a minute, close your eyes, and try to imagine someone you know doing that for you. He let his only child die, not just so you could live out your life on earth but also that you could live *forever*. Imagine how much you would love that person and how you would want to serve him and give him anything he needed.

That's how Jesus' sacrifice feels to me and I'm assuming to other believers as well. I know Jesus was a real human being who died on a cross and shed His blood, and because He did that, I know I will have eternal life in heaven. I know God sacrificed His only Son for me, so the love and gratitude I feel toward Him overcomes any personal want or need. His amazing grace rescued me, and I will forever love Him for that.

Chapter 15

Then Sings My Soul...

I would be remiss if I wrote an entire book about how God has transformed me and left out the impact of worship music. Singing praises to the Lord is written about throughout the Bible.

Oh come, let us sing to the Lord; let us make a joyful noise to the rock of our salvation! (Psalm 95:1).

Is anyone among you suffering? Let him pray. Is anyone cheerful? Let him sing praise (James 5:13).

I've always loved music. My favorite song when I was five years old was "Good Golly, Miss Molly." (My mom was a fan of an oldies radio station.) Music has always brought me peace and joy. I loved listening to music from the 1950s and '60s in the car with my mom. I loved listening to Queen and Aerosmith with my dad. One of my favorite memories as a kid is my dad, my brother, and me blasting "Play That Funky Music, White Boy" and singing at the top of our lungs. I love how music can take you right back to a specific memory. Jimmy Buffett always takes me back to sitting on the bow of our motorboat in the middle of a lake in North Carolina. Christmas piano music takes me back to cozy winter evenings as a family around the fireplace in our living room. Journey's "Don't Stop Believin'" takes me back to college, dancing with Michael on '80s night. I love the emotions that come from hearing particular songs. I love the camaraderie of singing familiar tunes together.

As I've grown closer to the Lord, my taste in music has changed, but the effect music has on me hasn't changed at all. I'd even say it's intensified. If I have a particularly rough day, I no longer crank up some Eminem and sing along to his angry lyrics to feel a sense of release. (Don't judge me. Many of us loved some Eminem back in the day.)

Now I crank the worship music. Of King and Country's "Joy" will turn my mood around on a bad day. I mean, who can listen to that song without smiling and wanting to jump up and boogie? My kids and I can have the *worst* ten minutes trying to get everyone out of the house for ballet and baseball, but if we get in the car and that song comes on, I can watch my kids in the back seat slowly start to smile, and by the end of the song, we're all singing at the top of our lungs.

After a few months of listening to only Christian radio in the car each day, I realized what a difference it was making. I started this daily habit during that tough year in Virginia, when I'd just had my third baby and felt overwhelmed and out of control. Those were some hard days, but once I started spending my time in the car listening to Christian music, things felt a little easier.

The messages in the songs left me feeling uplifted and closer to God. I can remember belting out certain lyrics while sobbing behind the wheel. I'm pretty sure my kids thought I was a crazy person. But those lyrics touched my heart in an incredible way. Even if God didn't take away my pain, I could still put all my hope in Him.

Any song about the cross will have me in tears every single time I hear it, no matter what mood I'm in. Passionately singing about the way Jesus died for us and saved us all overwhelms me *every time*. I've always been emotionally affected by love songs. In high school, I overplayed every sappy '90s love ballad ever written. This was back in the day of burning mix CDs, and I'm pretty sure I had a *five-CD set* of love songs that I made and played quite frequently. I felt as if those artists *knew* my teenage heartache and pain and had somehow put it into words. Now, I'm equally moved by the way Christian artists put God's love into words.

So many songs on Christian radio are clearly divinely inspired. Whether the song is meant to encourage you, sympathize with you, teach you, remind you—whatever the message is, it's always a message of the biggest love and hope imaginable. If you're afraid, there are countless songs on how to fight fear. If you're feeling hopeless, there are songs about trusting the Lord in all situations and finding hope in His promises. Some songs are as simple as stating a true belief in God, Jesus, and our salvation.

Praise God for Christian radio.

One of the best parts? My young kids are singing along! When I occasionally switch to a local country or rock station, I have to pay attention to what's being said and be ready to change the station when things get inappropriate, either in the song lyrics or during a talk segment. My three-year-old son's favorite game in the car right now is, "Mommy, what's this song about?" When it's a country song about a guy and girl meeting in a bar and heading home together for the night, I struggle to explain that one! But when it's a song about Jesus, I'm having a conversation about the holy Trinity and our salvation, just from a simple song on the radio.

These songs give us so many opportunities to talk about hope, love, mercy, grace, and eternity, not to mention all the valuable lessons learned when the DJs are talking. Radio hosts often tell uplifting stories or play games that teach biblical lessons. If you can't tell, I'm a huge fan of Christian radio.

Let's not forget about worship music at church. This is probably my favorite part of the week. I go to church every Sunday for a lot of reasons, but once I started attending churches that feature contemporary worship music, that easily became my favorite part. I love music, but I *love* to sing. Unfortunately, I can't carry a tune. I think of it as one of God's little jokes. He gave me a passion for music and a terrible voice. Hence my love of singing at church. Our church has a full rock band up on stage, and it's loud! I can sing at full volume, and no one notices! Plus, we're singing songs I actually know and love!

Before, in churches that used hymnals, I tried to read the music at the same time as the words in an attempt to figure out the tune. I got so excited when we sang a familiar hymn, but that seemed so rare! I'm not saying there is anything wrong with hymns. I love hymns. I know a lot of older people prefer hymns, but I think that's because they know the hymns, so they're easy for them to sing along to. I spent so much time just trying to figure out how to sing the song that I barely paid attention to the words. When we sing contemporary Christian songs at church and I know all or most of the words, I can pay attention to what I'm singing and feel the emotion of the words.

Yes, I've become a hands-in-the-air person during moving moments of the songs we sing. And I find many moments in most of the songs to be moving, so my hands are in the air quite a bit. First Timothy 2:8 says,

"I want men everywhere to <u>lift up holy hands</u> in prayer, without anger or disputing."

That's one of many verses about lifting your hands during times of prayer and praise.

I certainly don't think it's a requirement for properly worshipping the Lord, but if He moves you to raise your hands, don't be shy! I once had a good friend tell me she started lifting her hands while singing when she finally realized she should care more about what the Lord thinks than worrying about what those around her think. I admit that when I'm in a new church, I'm hesitant to lift my hands until I see at least one other person doing it. I've still got some work to do to overcome my inhibitions and let my love for the Lord come first. But I'm making progress.

I used to keep my hands down simply because I was afraid Michael would think I was crazy. He's much more reserved when it comes to something like that because he grew up in a more subdued church. But I eventually got over that fear of what he would think and put the Lord's opinion of me first. *This is not easy to do.* But I did it, thanks to God using my friend's wise advice about putting His perception of me above all others. And now I enjoy worship music even more, hands up and all.

Chapter 16

Our Daily Grace

*But he said to me, "My grace is sufficient
for you, for my power is made perfect in
weakness." Therefore I will boast all the more
gladly about my weaknesses, so that
Christ's power may rest on me.*
2 Corinthians 12:9

H is grace is sufficient for you. Did you fully read and comprehend that? *His grace is sufficient for you*. We've talked a lot about the struggles we can face daily as a wife and mother. We've also talked a lot about how Jesus gets me through those struggles. But I want to make sure you understand how important grace is in *your* day-to-day life.

The verse above, 2 Corinthians 12:9, has special meaning to me. When Michael first got sober and spent a couple of weeks in rehab, I was at home busily trying to prepare our house for this new way of life. Obviously, I was getting rid of any alcohol or anything that would remind Michael of alcohol, like wine glasses and corkscrews. I also wanted to strategically place helpful scripture verses around the house that would encourage Michael when he was feeling tempted or discouraged. The problem was that I was a new Christian and knew little about scripture or how to look in the Bible for something relevant to a specific issue.

I called my dad and asked for his help. He gave me 2 Corinthians 12:9, which I printed on a 5-by-7 sheet of paper, framed, and put in our bathroom. It stayed in our bathroom for years, so I read it pretty much every day. I even tried to memorize it for a while, as I brushed my teeth each night. But as I've mentioned, I'm *terrible* at memorization, and it never stuck. I can tell you the gist of it if you ask me, though. But I probably would forget which book it is in.

I don't know if Michael ever turned to that verse in times of trouble, but it always comforted me, especially in those early days of sobriety when I was having trouble trusting that Michael had changed. I'd see that verse in my bathroom and be reminded that Michael's weaknesses—and mine—deserve grace, because they only bring us closer to the Lord. And as we overcome those weaknesses, it brings glory to the Lord.

As Christians, we're supposed to model our lives after Jesus, right? Many of us disagree on what that means when it comes to a lot of hot-button topics. But when it comes to love and kindness and grace, I don't think there's much to disagree about. Love your neighbor. The end. No conditions. It doesn't say, "Love your neighbor as long as they never do anything to annoy or upset you." It certainly doesn't say, "Love your neighbor unless they're from the other political party." (Insert eye-roll emoji.)

We are called to live as Jesus did, and Jesus loved all His neighbors. I'd also like to point out that "neighbors" doesn't just mean the people who live next door. I'm pretty sure that also includes your family. Your spouse. Your children. I find it so easy to give grace to the stranger who cut me off in traffic or didn't hold the door as I followed them out of a building. I assume they have a reason for being in a hurry or they need some kind of change of heart, and I try to remember to pray for them. Why is it so much harder to give that same grace to my kids when they do something not very nice? Or to Michael? For some reason, I have to work twice as hard to give my family the same kind of grace I extend to strangers. But I'm pretty sure my family is included in the whole "neighbors" thing. When Jesus said to love them, that includes giving them grace.

Think about the adulterous woman who was brought before Jesus in John 8. The crowd wanted to stone her for her sin, according to the law of Moses. His response to her sin?

"Let any one of you who is without sin be the first to throw a stone at her" (John 8:7).

Then He told the woman He did not condemn her and that she should go and leave her life of sin. What a great example of grace and how it brings about something new!

Jesus could have condemned her for her sin, but instead He gave her grace and another shot at living a better life. We love our children so much that we would die for them. But are we living out that love on a daily basis? Sure, we feed and clothe and shelter them, and occasionally get down on the floor and play painstakingly boring games just to put a smile on their faces. But if we're not extending grace to them for their mistakes, what kind of love are we showing them? We also need to model how to give grace to ourselves.

I am perfectly aware when I yell at one of my kids for no good reason. It could be because I'm tired, hungry, or just in a cranky mood, but that doesn't ever justify flying off the handle. One of the best things we can do in that situation is humble ourselves before our kids. It usually looks something like this:

Five-year-old Kelly is sniffling and wiping away tears. I just screamed at her to pick up her shoes, because I'd asked her to do it fifteen times, and they were still in the middle of the floor. She quietly picks up her shoes and looks at me with watery eyes and a bottom lip sticking out. Sometimes my heart melts right at that moment, and I pull her in my arms, ready to apologize. Sometimes five or ten minutes go by, I walk away and cool down and then realize I made a bad choice, out of unrighteous anger.

Either way, I go to Kelly, apologize for getting so mad, and tell her, "Mommy is human. I'm not perfect, and I mess up too. I have to ask God for help just like you do, so I'm going to pray and ask Him to help me not get mad so easily." Kelly still needs to be disciplined for not picking her shoes up the first time I told her to, but I don't think any harm is done by showing her that I went about the discipline in the wrong way. I'm hoping it teaches her that she will *always* need God's help, even when she grows up, and that it's OK to ask Him for His help. Maybe it will help her start to understand God's grace.

This is something I have to remind myself almost daily. It's challenging to find the line between being permissive and giving grace. And there are much better Christian parenting experts out there than me. I don't have it all figured out. This parenting thing is really hard! But I do know what I'm striving for. I may not know how to get there, but I know where I want to go and what I *need* to get there. I want to be the kind of parent Jesus would be, and I need His love, strength, and grace to get there.

Whew, that's a lot to strive for as a parent! But don't relax yet. We also need to strive for this in our marriages. Grace has been a saving grace in my marriage. Grace and humility. When I mess up, I need Michael to show me some grace, and I need to humble myself and admit my wrongdoing. And vice versa. Y'all, this has made a world of difference.

As we started walking with the Lord (at different paces, mind you), God softened our hearts toward one another. We loved each other, but we had this hard layer of pride around our hearts that made it hard for anything else to get in. I say "we" because I believe we both had this problem in equal measure. But God also healed it in equal measure, around the time our first child was born.

Suddenly, not every fight was to the death. Suddenly, we weren't so blinded by our own point of view that it was impossible to sympathize with each other. We became a team that wanted to fight *for* each other, not against each other. If I'm having a crabby day, Michael has learned that it's probably caused by our three little hooligans, and he can sympathize with that. So instead of reacting to my crabbiness with hostility or annoyance, he tries to comfort me and ease some of the stress. Or if we get in a fight over something (because that still happens; walking with the Lord does not mean you never get in disagreements), we can find our way out of it pretty quickly.

We're much more likely to listen to each other's opinions and feelings and try to understand them than we were in the past. There's a level of love and respect there that translates into grace when one of us misses the mark when it comes to being a good spouse. I can only attribute that to God. It was such an abrupt change of heart for both of us that it could only be the work of our heavenly Father, who wanted us to be in this for the long haul. It was a huge part of the equation that saved our relationship.

I need to insert some truth here though. Our marriage is not perfect or happy all the time. I don't want you to misunderstand me and think that if you and your husband are going through a rough time, you must be getting it all wrong. Michael and I still have times when we forget this whole grace thing, and a dark cloud settles over us for a while. It can last a couple of hours, a couple of days, or a couple of weeks. We're human, and the enemy fights dirty. When Satan sees us rocking this whole "love, respect, and grace" thing, he comes at us hard. Sometimes it takes us a little while to realize it's happening. I usually realize it faster if my prayer life is on point. But if Satan's attacks come when I'm not spending as much time with the Lord as I should—oh boy, we're in for it! And that happens.

Michael and I will sometimes have a week or two when we're very cranky with one another for no good reason, nagging at each other every day. Eventually, we realize something is amiss, and one of us will start the fun conversation of "what's going on with us?" I'm happy to say we've reached a point where one of us brings that up eventually. We don't let too much time go by before one of us is brave enough to start the conversation that leads back to sunshine in our marriage.

I believe that's all God's handiwork. He's helped us both grow, especially in our interaction with the Holy Spirit, and we can feel Him nudging us to check in with one another and try to get back on track. Getting back on track usually leads to a conversation about how one of us wronged the other one, and that's when grace and humility come into play to start the healing.

Clothe yourselves, all of you, with humility toward one another, for "God opposes the proud but gives grace to the humble" (1 Peter 5:5).

Chapter 17

Get on Your Knees

One of my favorite sayings is, "I still remember the days I prayed for the things I have now." My prayer life is one of the most important parts of my life. None of the other parts—my family life, fitness life, married life, work life—none of it works if my prayer life isn't intact. This is something I did not realize until the last couple of years. Growing up, I thought praying was something you did before bed every night, when you listed every member of your family you could think of and asked God to bless them. As I got older, I didn't even pray before bedtime anymore. I probably only prayed if something awful was happening and maybe not even then.

Right before the Lord called me back to Him, I *was* praying every night. I was desperate for help to get out of my situation, and something told me to call on God. I wasn't walking with Him, but I was turning to Him to rescue me. Once He did rescue me, my prayer life faded away again. It wasn't until I was regularly reading my Bible and being around other people who prayed that I realized the importance of daily conversations with the Lord. It's the only way to build a true relationship with Him.

> *Rejoice always, pray continually, give thanks in all circumstances, for this is God's will for you in Christ Jesus* (1 Thessalonians 5:16-18).

> *Do not be anxious about anything, but in everything by prayer and supplication with thanksgiving let your requests be made known to God* (Philippians 4:6).

> *And whatever you ask in prayer, you will receive, if you have faith* (Matthew 21:22).

I included all three of those verses because they each contribute a different perspective on praying, and they all helped to shape my current prayer life. We are supposed to pray continually, about everything. That means a constant conversation with God. That word "conversation" is what really changed things for me.

I'd always thought of prayer as something so official that it had to be stated a certain way. I mean, you are talking to the God of the entire universe, right? That must require a certain kind of speech. But as I grew in my relationship with God and came to know Him as my Father, I realized I was dead wrong. He is our Father. How do you talk to your dad? I doubt you're all stuffy and formal sounding. Your dad is probably someone you can be honest and vulnerable with. That's how I came to view God. Like a father and a best friend, someone I could tell anything to (He knows all of it anyway), and someone I could ask for help with anything.

I started having conversations with God throughout my day, as if I were talking to a friend who was standing right beside me. I talk to the Lord every morning when I study the Bible. Then I talk to Him in the car when I'm taking the kids to school. I talk to Him when I'm in the shower, when I'm washing the dishes, when I run the vacuum. It feels so much more like a true relationship when I talk to God that often. The prayers become conversational, and I can be totally honest, since God is the only one listening. It was only after I started conversing with Him all throughout the day that I started feeling the guidance of the Holy Spirit, and it definitely takes away some of the loneliness that can come with being a stay-at-home mom. Before I knew it, I was seeing answered prayers, and my relationship with the Lord was growing.

God also commands us to "not be anxious about anything." Easier said than done, right? Especially for those of us prone to anxiety over all things, big and small. He wants us to give all anxiety to Him and trust Him to take care of the situation. This is a hard one for me, because what if God's will for a situation is what I'm feeling anxiety about? What if I'm anxious about a job interview because I'm afraid I won't get the job? I pray and cast those anxieties on the Lord in hopes that He will secure the job for me, and then if I still don't get the job, that's because it wasn't part of God's plan.

It's been a long road for me to accept that, but I've come to understand that everything should be about bringing glory to the Lord. Maybe He doesn't want me to get that job because being unemployed is going to cause me to lean on Him more. In turn, my relationship with Him will grow and my testimony will get stronger. That could eventually bring someone else to know Christ, meaning it's better that I didn't get the job. It can be hard to not be short-sighted, though. The Chrissie of today needs the job and can't see a future where everything works out for good. But

"We know that in all things God works for the good of those who love him, who have been called according to his purpose" (Romans 8:28).

Nothing is better than God's perfect plan for us.

We can cast our anxieties on Him and trust that He will take care of us, whether that means getting a job now or staying in the unemployment line a little longer. Through "prayer and supplication with thanksgiving let your requests be made known to God." "Supplication" means asking for something earnestly or humbly. Don't be afraid to beg God for help. He wants us to come to Him rather than taking control ourselves or letting our anxieties eat us alive.

I also have learned about the importance of praying outside your own circle of needs. James 5:16 says,

"Therefore, confess your sins to one another and pray for one another; that you may be healed. The prayer of a righteous person has great power as it is working."

When I began spending every morning with the Lord, I got a prayer journal that guided me on each day's Bible reading and prayer time. In addition to the daily Bible lesson, it included a certain person or place to pray for each day of the week. On Mondays, I pray for a specific family member. On Tuesdays, I pray for a friend. On Wednesdays, I pray for our church and its leaders. On Thursday, I pray for our country and its leaders. On Friday, I pray for an impoverished or war-scarred country. And so on.

Those daily prayers for others opened my eyes to the power of prayer, especially when I wasn't praying for someone I knew. Could my simple prayer at my kitchen table make a difference to someone sheltering their family from bombs being dropped in a war-torn country? Of course it can, because God said,

"And whatever you ask in prayer, you will receive, if you have faith" (Matthew 21:22).

I have to pause here and address this "whatever you ask for, you receive" thing, because it confused me at first so I'm going to assume it's tripped up some of you as well, especially if you're a nonbeliever. For me, this verse doesn't mean you can ask for a million dollars, and God will give it to you. I also don't think it means I can sit at my table and pray for a war to end, and the bombs will suddenly stop dropping. That's not how it works, and I'm not going to pretend that I know exactly how it works. But I'm pretty sure your heart has to be in the right place for your prayer to be answered. And God always knows where our hearts lie.

Am I asking for a million dollars because I'd like to instantly be debt-free and never have to worry about money again? God's probably not going to give me that, because then I wouldn't learn how to trust Him to provide for me in all circumstances. That wouldn't line up with His will for me. If I was asking for a million dollars so I could start a charity to benefit foster children? He might just answer that prayer in one way or another.

I've seen Him answer monetary prayers like that in which someone needed a specific amount of money, prayed for it, and God gave them that exact amount of money. I believe when that happens, you know your plan for that money 100 percent lines up with God's plan. God definitely answers some crazy prayers in crazy ways, and it all brings glory to Him when those stories are shared!

Back when I was in college, I came across a website that said the state could owe you money for one reason or another. You plugged in your name, and it would tell you if any money was owed to you and how to claim it. I tried my own name and didn't come up with anything, which was frustrating because I was a poor college student. But something told me to try my dad's name as well. It showed the state of Florida owed him somewhere around $2,500!

For the sake of the story, let's say it was $2,497. I can't remember why he was owed this money, but nevertheless, it was his. I immediately called him and told him about it. Turns out, he was in need of a car and had just found a good used car that was being sold for exactly $2,497. No joke, the cost of the car was to the penny, exactly the amount of money I had just found out he was owed! He had been praying for God to get him that money somehow, and God answered that prayer very specifically. He didn't give Dad a raise at work so he could earn the money over time. He just handed Dad the exact amount he needed at that moment. God will answer monetary prayers if the need is real. Dad drove that car for years and called it the "God car."

The saying I started with, "I remember the days I prayed for the things I have now," brings about an attitude of gratitude, and that changed my prayer life too. Gratitude is easy when things are looking good. It's natural to thank God for healthy kids, a loving husband, plenty of food, a nice house, good friends, and sunny weather. But I haven't always remembered to thank God for the good stuff.

For a long time, my prayers consisted of asking God *for* things, as if He was some kind of genie in a bottle. I complained about my problems and asked for help. Or I complained on behalf of someone else and asked Him to help them. It took some time for me to recognize the importance of thanking God for my blessings. Motherhood helped me get there.

It can be frustrating when I've spent an entire day taking care of my kids' laundry or an entire afternoon cooking them a delicious meal, and I get no appreciation for it. One day I realized God may feel that way too. He blesses us in a million different ways every day, most of the time when we didn't even ask for it. The least we can do is thank Him for that!

I love the innocence of my kids. When asked what they want to thank God for each night, they say the simplest things, like "I want to thank God for letting me go to school today" or "I want to thank God for the flowers." We all could learn a thing or two from little ones. It creates such a warm feeling of happiness in your heart when you take time to thank God for all the blessings, big and small. It's hard to stay sad when you're listing all the good things in your life. If you're having trouble thinking of anything good, just thank Him for the breath in your lungs, the blood in your veins, and the chance to see another day.

An even harder lesson for me was learning to show gratitude in the hard times. It's simply not easy to say, "Thank You for this tough situation." But I recently read two things that helped put this concept into perspective.

"Thanking God during good times is a natural response, but thanking Him in a difficult situation is an act of the will. I'm impressed with the lesson one intercessor friend shared with me about trustful thanks. If I had a flat tire, I would thank God that it was in my driveway rather than on some deserted stretch of road or that it hadn't been a blowout on the highway. But God started convicting me that I was thanking Him around the situation—not for the situation itself. He pointed out that He would not have permitted these particular situations unless they could perfect me. They were refining fire. They actually were answers to prayers, for I had been praying for a deeper walk and to be a purer vessel."—Brenda Poinsett, *Pray!* magazine

I've heard Christians say you should never pray for patience, because then the Lord will bring to you a hard situation to help you practice how to be patient! I think that's the point being made in the passage above. The hard situations are the ones that teach us how to rely on God, how to cast all our worries on Him, and how to trust that He is in control and will provide. This is not easy. I repeat, *this is not easy*.

For a control freak like me, this is difficult and requires daily reminders. In my heart, I know and believe that God has my back all the time, but my brain forgets that regularly and tries to take the reins. It's something I'm working on and want to overcome. I'm thankful for the tough situations God uses to bring me closer to full reliance on Him.

The next passage I want to share is about finding gratitude during tragedy. I'm not just talking about one of those bad days when nothing seems to go right. I mean a genuine tragedy. How do we find gratitude in those times?

> "Praying during times of tragedy can be difficult. Sometimes we just don't know how to pray. And that's when we take comfort that the Holy Spirit intercedes on our behalf 'with groans that words cannot express.' How might we thank God during difficult times? We can thank God that the enemy has made a tactical error, since God will use for good what Satan has intended for harm (Genesis 50:20-21). Thank Him for the people who will be drawn to seek God's face because the overwhelming nature of the tragedy leaves them nowhere else to turn."—Lani Hinkle and Sandra Higley, *Pray!* magazine

There is so much comfort in that! God gave us the wonderful gift of the Holy Spirit, who will speak to God on our behalf when we don't know what to say, when things are so bad that we can't even come up with the words. God doesn't need us to verbalize our needs. He will bring comfort and answer prayers in the worst of times, if we just turn to Him. He uses it all for good! Satan can throw his worst at us, and God will still turn it around for good. It's so inspirational to see the people who have been able to overcome a tragedy using this mindset.

Pray then like this: "Our Father, who art in heaven, hallowed be your name. Your kingdom come, your will be done, on earth as it is in heaven. Give us this day our daily bread, and forgive us our debts, as we also have forgiven our debtors. And lead us not into temptation but deliver us from evil" (Matthew 6:9-13).

Chapter 18

Daughters of the King

Learning to live by grace is not an easy thing to do, but it's what we're called to do. It requires a fundamental change of thinking about who we are. I listened to a podcast recently by Rachel Faulkner Brown, who talked about viewing yourself as a daughter of the King, not as a sinner. When I first started walking with the Lord and read Romans 3:23—"For all have sinned and fall short of the glory of God"—I'm pretty sure that resonated with me because for a long time I'd viewed myself as a sinner and nothing more.

I had years of bad choices under my belt, and the guilt weighed heavily on me. I saw myself as a saved sinner but still a sinner. My brain understood that God forgave all those sins when I accepted Jesus as my Savior and asked for forgiveness, but my heart didn't *feel* His forgiveness. I still felt as if I wasn't good enough to share an inheritance with Christ. My past mistakes had been erased from God's memory but not from my memory.

Then I heard a pastor say that we don't have the right to bring up our past sins. If God did something as monumental as sacrificing His only Son to forgive our sins, how dare we minimize that by dwelling on the sins that have been forgiven? That was a real lightbulb moment for me. I could let go of my mistakes because I didn't have a right to dwell on them.

That is, I could let go of most of my mistakes. There were still a couple of things I couldn't seem to stop feeling guilty about, and I couldn't figure out what was holding me back. Why was I being held captive by these old sins? Where was this freedom in Christ I'd heard so much about? I started praying about being able to let go, and God showed me the word "repent." I hadn't asked for forgiveness specifically for these sins I couldn't get over. I think it was the part about acknowledging the sin out loud, or silently to God, that was tripping me up, which is ridiculous, because God already knows all that I've done. But let me tell you, once I finally took the step of repentance, the guilt was washed away. I was free of my past. Don't skip over the repentance part on the road to receiving God's amazing grace.

Eventually, through several Bible studies and vulnerable conversations with other believers, I learned how deep God's love goes, and I finally started to feel like a daughter of the King. That's such a huge change in perspective, to go from thinking of yourself as merely a sinner to thinking of yourself as a *daughter*.

Responsible parents don't view their children as these bad little humans who never get anything right. Good parents love their children unconditionally and give them that much-needed grace when they inevitably mess up. We're talking about *human* parents here, and we have it in our capacity to forgive our children every time they do something wrong. Now imagine how powerful our God, the Creator of the universe, is and how much grace and forgiveness He extends to us as our Father. That is something you can always count on. God is forever faithful and never goes back on His promise to forgive our sins, thanks to Jesus' death on the cross.

Being a daughter of the King not only comes with grace and forgiveness; more importantly, it also comes with an amazing inheritance. We're not just talking about Aunt Susie's pearls. A daughter of the King has an *equal* inheritance with Christ.

Now if we are children, then we are heirs of God and co-heirs with Christ, if indeed we share in his sufferings in order that we may also share in his glory (Romans 8:17).

That is something that can't be taken away. No matter how many times you mess up, God will forgive you, and your inheritance is intact. Accepting Jesus as your Savior guarantees this. As I said earlier, accepting Jesus doesn't have to be this dramatic moment in the middle of a church service. It *can* be a dramatic moment in a church service. But it can also be a quiet moment in your bedroom or driving down the street or in the shower.

The time and place don't matter to the Lord. He just wants you to invite Him into your life. I'd even go as far as to say it doesn't have to be a specific "moment" at all. Most people I know have had that moment, but I didn't. It was much more of a gradual process for me, as if I was slowly stepping out of the shadows. One day I realized I was fully in the light, walking hand in hand with Jesus, and my eternity was secure.

And with that eternal salvation comes a heaping dose of God's grace.

So when you have to make your fourth trip to the grocery store this week because you can't seem to remember to get everything *even when it's on the list*, give yourself grace. Or better yet, accept the grace God is giving you for not being perfect.

When you scream like a banshee at your five-year-old because you've told her to put her shoes on fifteen times, squash that mom guilt, apologize, and accept the grace God is giving you.

When you snap at your husband for no good reason and cause a three-day fight, humble yourself and accept the grace God is giving you.

If we could all remember that five letter word, G-R-A-C-E, our lives would be a lot lighter and a lot closer to how the Lord wants us to be living.

And remember, you can always name your daughter Grace so you'll be reminded of the word each time you yell at her.

Acknowledgments

How do you thank everyone who is a part of something like this? It would take an endless number of pages to thank each person who contributed to this book and all the stories in it. But I do find it important to publicly thank a few of you.

To my husband, Michael – your unwavering support of everything I do is the reason I can find the strength to keep going, especially on the hard days. I'm in awe of your courage and faith in allowing me to share your story as part of mine. I'm so grateful God brought us together and *kept* us together so we could create this beautiful life. I don't know what I'd do without your love, friendship, and willingness to listen to me explain my spaghetti brain on a daily basis!

I want to thank my kids, Kelly, Clayton, and Ava, for inspiring so much of this book. Some days I can hardly believe I get to be your mom. Your vibrant personalities and kind spirits inspire me daily. Thank you for cooperating with the long hours that I spent working on this book, away from you. I hope the lessons I've shared here will inspire you all one day.

To my parents – thank you for raising me to know Jesus and understand the value of God's Word. I may not have started following Him until I became an adult, but you sowed the seed that helped me get there.

A big shout-out goes to the people who read my book first and helped me find the courage to bring it to the world – Becky, Danny, and Jeanne. You all contributed valuable insights and helped me shape this into something I love.

To Sara Anna Powers, my mentor and friend – thank you for your continued kindness and support. I wouldn't be sharing my story with the world without your help! I appreciate your role in making this happen, and I look forward to all the things in our future.

To Angie Kiesling and Marcia Ford at The Editorial Attic – thank you so much for your editorial genius! You played a crucial role in bringing this book to life.

To Gayle West, Jim Howard, David Hancock, and the entire team at Morgan James Publishing – thank you for helping this new author make her dreams come true and bring her testimony of God's grace to the world.

Lastly, I want to thank you, the reader, for taking a chance on someone you've most likely never heard of. I'm grateful that you read my story, and I pray it helps you get a little closer to Jesus in your daily life. No more #momguilt, y'all!

About the Author

C hrissie Kenaston's love for writing blossomed in the sixth grade, when her teacher began each day with a one-sentence story prompt on the chalkboard. The students would write a one-page story from that prompt every morning. Chrissie immediately fell in love with the craft.

But her love was torn between writing and ballet, and she chose to passionately pursue the dance world through high school and into college. She never stopped writing, though, keeping journals and notebooks full of thoughts and dreams over the years.

Halfway through college, it became clear that her dance dreams would not be fulfilled, so she switched gears and obtained a mass media degree, going on to work as a television news producer right out of college.

After four years in the TV world, God changed her path again as she married a military man and began a life that involved moving every two to three years. Full-time motherhood became her job as she birthed three beautiful children while they moved around the world.

Chrissie always knew the Lord but strayed from Him for many years. He called her back to His arms after the birth of her first child, and her life has never been the same.

She's seen firsthand the power of having a real relationship with our heavenly Father and the transformation that comes when we allow His grace into our lives.

Chrissie wrote *What If I Name Her Grace?* in just thirty days. The words flowed easily as she recounted the many ways God moved in her life and molded her into the wife, mother, daughter, sister, and friend she is today. She believes God wants to use her words to share a powerful message of love, forgiveness, and grace.

Chrissie is married to Michael, and together they have three children, Kelly, Clayton, and Ava. They currently live in New Mexico, but they move every two years, as most military families do, so who knows where they'll be living when you read this book?

Chrissie was born in North Carolina, but Florida will always feel like home. She feels the most peace when near a body of water. And has the most fun when she's cheering on her beloved Seminoles of Florida State University.